Ninety Six District, South Carolina

Journal of the Court of Ordinary

Inventory Book
Will Book
1781-1786

By
Brent H. Holcomb, G. R. S.

All Rights Reserved. No part of this publication may be reproduced, stored in a retrieval system or transmitted in any form or by any means without the prior written permission of the publisher.

Please direct ALL correspondence and book orders to:
Southern Historical Press, Inc.
PO Box 1267
375 West Broad Street
Greenville, SC 29602-1267
www.southernhistoricalpress.com

ISBN #0-89308-109-4

Printed in the United States of America

INTRODUCTION

The volume herein transcribed and abstracted is in the Office of the Probate Judge, Abbeville County Court House, Abbeville, South Carolina. It was originally two separate books. The first was a combination Journal of the Ordinary and Inventory book. The other was a will book. These books were combined when lamenated some years ago. The Journal has been called "Pat Calhoun's Surrogate Court Book" and various other titles, none of which are really accurate. John Ewing Colhoun was appointed Ordinary for Ninety Six District by proclamation of Governor John Rutledge November 3, 1781. Patrick Calhoun, who called himself Surrogate, apparently acted for him . Probably the proper term should have been Deputy Ordinary, rather than Surrogate. The Journal part of this book is similar to the Journal of the Ordinary of the Province, 1771-1775, transcribed by me, and publisehd in Probate Records of South Carolina, Volume II. There are, however, some basic differences. The entries are made day by day, but space was left for later entries concerning the same estate proceeding. This is evident in the original by spaces left wherein there was no further proceeding, and also by later entries in different handwriting. The actual entries stop March 31, 1783 for new estates, but additions were made in the book up until 1786. By February 10, 1783, John Thomas Junr had been appointed Ordinary for Ninety Six District. However, it appears that the office of John Ewing Colhoun still continued to function. There may have been two courts of ordinary in Ninety Six District for a time. John Thomas Junr probably held court at his plantation in what was later Spartanburg County. He continued as ordinary until 1787, when probates became the jurisdiction of the county courts which were set up in 1785. The counties formed in Ninety Six District were Abbeville, Edgefield, Laurens, Spartanburg, Newberry, Union and Greenville (1786).

There are references in the journal entries to the pages where the inventories are recorded. Unfortunately, this book was already in poor condition at the time of lamentation. There are several whole pages missing and parts of pages destroyed. Brackets ([]) are used for editorial remarks and to show words which were still legible when the WPA copy was made, but are no longer legible or are now entirely missing. The WPA copy was carefully compared with the original for this reason. Brackets are also used to show words or lines now entirely missing. ([   ]). The journal portion of the book is a verbatim transcription. All wills and inventories are abstracted, with the exception of the will of the Indian agent, George Galphin; because it is historically important, it is transcribed verbatim.

The contents of this journal are valuable from a genealogical and historical point. Some estates are mentioned for which no original papers have survived. A few marriage licenses are found scattered through the journal. Some wills and estates from a period prior to this journal were recorded here, because of the difficulties in Charleston(where all probates were recorded before 1781) during the Revolution. The statements concerning the estate of John Williams (original pages 65-66) are indicative of this. The law of primogeniture (in force in South Carolina until 1791) does not appear to have been well understood. By this law, all real estate became the property of the eldest son of the deceased intestate. Therefore, any appraisement of property in an inventory was unnecessary. Apparently, some appraisers were not aware of this face. Notice the entry on original page 59, and other similar ones, "land no right to be appraised." There is at least one will of which the original has not survived, but is recorded here: the will of William Golightly. This will has not appeared in other published abstracts. (The will of his widow Amey Golightly has been abstracted and published in my Some County Records of South Carolina, Volume I.)

          Brent H. Holcomb, G. R. S.
          Columbia, South Carolina
          August 3, 1977

[Page 1 missing]

2	[1781]	[Decr] 22d	John Wardlaw took a Citation on Estate of Wm. McCluer Deceased-- 28th Decr published by Revd. Mr. Harris
		Do 28th	took out Letters of Administration as highest creditor, on Estate of said William McCluer--Didimus to Wm. Moore to swear appraisers--Bail Bond, ₤ 1000 sterling Penalty-- Security Wm. Brown, Alexdr. Noble Septr. 24th, John Wardlaw Admin, returnd into the Ordinarys Office an Inventory & appraist, and the Sales of the Estate of Wm. McCluer deceased-- (Mr. Wardlaw saith he did not know Sooner that any one was appointed in the ordinarys office in J. E. Calhouns absence to make a return to) Recorded in page 91 of this Book
		Decr	John Strain and Robert Bond, Citation on Estate of Thomas Strain, Deceased
		Decr. 31	Said John Strain & Robt. Bond took Letters of Administration, as next of Kin, on Estate of said Thomas Strain--Swore appraisers myself Bail Bond, ₤ 1000 Proclamation Mony of America, Penalty--Security said administrators and William Drennan & Samuel McMurtray--
		April 23d	John Strain Administrator returned into the Ordinary's Office an Inventory & appraisemt. of the personal Estate of Thomas Strain, deceased. Recorded in pages 99 & 100 of this Book

[Part of the dates in this column missing]

		9th	Sarah Moore took Citation on Estate of John Moore, deceased, Rev. Mr. Harris published 30th Decr.
		th	Said Sarah Moore took Letters of Administration as Widow & Next of Kin, of Estate of said John Moore, deceased Sworn Appraisers myself Bail Bond, ₤ 1500 Proclamation Money of America, Penalty Security said Admix, Williss Breazeal and Peter Stubbs
		3d	Sarah Moore, Administratrix returned into the Ordinary's Office an Inventory & appraisemt. of Estate of said John Moore deceased, [Recor]ded in page 93 of this Book
			[James] Baskins & Prudence Crawford, took [out Marriage] Licence and at same time [ ] Bond, Penalty ₤ 200 proclamation money--said James Baskins and Alexdr. Noble Securities
3	1782		
		Jany. 4th	William McMaster took Citation on Estate John & Patrick McMaster, deceased, --7th Jany published by the Revd. Mr. Harris.
		11th Do.	William McMaster took Letters of Administration as next of Kin, on Estate of John & Patrick McMaster deceased---Dedimes to Patrick Colhoun Esqr. to swear appraisers Viz. Wm McKinley, James Little, Wm. Hays & Robt Boyd---

Administration Bond, penalty ₺ 2000 proclamation Money of America, Security Wm. McKinley & Wm. Hays Appraisers sworn William McKinley, James Little, William Hays & Robert Boyd, before Pat: Calhoun, Esqr. The above power of appraist. Elapsed, New power granted the 30th July 1782. Inventory & appraist. filed 2d Septr.
Recorded in page 94 of this Book

April 16th   Arthur Patton took Citation on Estate of Samuel Patton, deceased--filed 22d April 1782

22d Do.   Arthur Patton took Letters of Administration as next of Kin of Estate of Samuel Patton, deceased, qualified James Noble, Peter Stubbs, & Wm Hays appraisers--Administration Bond, Security James Noble & Wm Hays, Penalty ₺ 2000 sterling--Septr 2d 1782 (appraisment not returned as prescribed by law) New Warrant of appraisment Granted; Inventory & appraisment filed in the Ordinary's office the 3d of Septr 1782. The Sale of Said Estate filed in the ordinary's Office the 10th of Octr. 1782. Recorded in page 97 of this book.

The last Will and Testament of George Galphin of Silver Bluff, executed the 6th day of April Anno Dom: 1776--Executors, James Parsons, John Graham, Lauchlin McGillvery, Esquires, John Parkinson Merhts. the said George, Thomas & John Galphins & William Dunbar and the Survivors or Survivor of them Executors of said last Will and Testament and of three several Codicils thereunto annexed--- John Sturzennegger one of the Witnesses to said Will made Oath, the 6th April 1782, that he saw the Testator George Galphin Sign Seal & properly execute the same & that David Zubly & Michal Meyer were also Witnesses to the Same Clotworthy Robson who was also a Witness to each of the three Codicils, saw the Testator George Galphin sign Seal & the same and Jonah Horry & David Zubly sign their Names as Witnesses to the first & that he saw William Harding & Richd Henderson sign their Names as Witnesses to the 2nd Codicil and that he saw John Anderson and Michal Walsh sign their Names as Witnesses to the third Codicil
the said 6th of April 1782. granted Warrant of appraismt. and qualify, Stephen Smith, Robt. Hankinson, and Alexdr. Newman appraisers---
said Thomas & George Galphin, qualified as Executors & Wm Dunbar
Farther proceedings [   ]
11th New Warrant of appraisment [   ]

4   [1782]   John Dick, his last Will & Testament executed 21st day of April Anno Dom. 1776, was probated in Ordinary's Office the 8th day of April 1782 by Alexdr. Newman a Subscribing witness--the other Witnesses Ann & John Newman.
Mary Dick, widow, appointed Executrix, qualifyed as such--Joseph Dick, son, the other Executor not qualifyed--Warrant of Appraisement given & Dedimus directed to Wm Dunbar Esqr to qualify such appraisers--26th Novr. 1782 Renewed the Warrant of appraismt. 21st December 1782, said Warrant of Appraismt and Inventory Returned into Ordinary's office---

Recorded in page 76 of this Book

April 9th	Mrs Christian Ardeis, Relict & widow of Mathias Ardies deceased, puts in her Caveat against any Person Administering on the Estate of the said Matthias Ardeis, untill she can have a hearing-- as she has not only a right to Administration, but is left the sole Executrix in a Will made, but cannot at present be probated one of the Witnesses being dead, & the other two now with the Enemy N. B. no farthr proceed in this office
Feby 12th	N. Milling enters a Caveat against any Person or Persons whatsoever obtaining Letters of Administration untill he can have a proper hearing--the Estate of Andrew Burney deceased, of Beach Island--Will Since probated & Letters Testamentory granted.
4th May	John Wyld Esqr enters a Caveat against any Person geting Admon on Estate of James McGill, untill he can have a hearg. Will produced & probated in the Ordinary's office the 9th of May 1782. See page 23d of this Book

5

The last Will & Testamt. of Robt. Boyd deceased, dated 21st day of April 1776, was probated in the Ordinary's office 20th April 1782 by Robt. Boyd Junr a subscribing Witness the other Witness Patrick McMaster dead, Wm. Hays appointed Ex & qualifyed as such, qualifyed myself the appraisers Viz Moses Davis, Wm. McKeer & Arther Morrow

Inventory & appraist, filed in the Ordinary's office the 27th July 1782.
Recorded in page 70 of this Book & page 71.
   amot. of Apprist. ₤ 162 11.

The last Will & Testament of James Adams dated 14th Octr 1781 was probated in the Ordinary's office the 26th April 1782 by Benjn. Moseley, a subscribing Witness--the other witnesses John Herndon, John Golding & hanah Mosely--Drury Adams appointed Ezor & qualifyed as such. Thomas Adams Ex not qualifyed Warrant of appraisemt. given & Dedimus to William Jones Esqr. to qualify appraisers

Inventory & appraist. filed in the Ordinary's office the 26th July 1782. Amount ₤ 3708 15
Recorded in page 69 of this Book

Recorded
in pages
36 & 37
of this Book

The last Will & Testamt. of James Norrel dated 12th August 1779 was probated in this Ordinary's Office 26th April 1782 by Richd. Allison subscribg. Witness. the other Witnesses William Anderson & Samuel Abney. Nathl. Spraggins & Isaac Norrel Exors & qualifyed as such--Mary Norrel his Wife Extx not qualified. Dedimus to John Wyld Esqr to qualify appraisers. N. B. The Warrant of appraise Elapsed, New Wart. of appraist. granted the 16th Septr. 1782 & a Dedimus to John Wyld & William Moore Esqrs to Swear appraisers--Inventory & appraisement Returned and filed in the ordinary's office the 16th Decr 1782.

3

	April 26th	Mary Derborough took Citation on Estate of Benjn. Derborough deceased. filed 3d. of May
	3d May	Said Mary Derborough took Dedimus to Wm. Moore Esqr to qualify her as Admix. & to Swears appraisers Inventory & appraisment in 3 sheets filed in the ordinary's office the 5th September 1782. Recorded in pages 77 & 78 of this Book.
	23d April	Citation to Binjn Tutt on Estate Saml. Williams filed 26th April
	27th Do.	Said Benjn. Tutt took Letters of Admon, as highest Creditor of Estate of said Saml. Williams--Dedimus to J. Purves Esqr to Swear appraisers-- Admon Bond ₤ 2000 Sterling Penalty. Security Wm. Moore & Josh. Towles. N. B. No Inventory, appraisment, nor Sale of the above Estate Returned to this Office.
6	April 20	Citation to B. Tutt on Estate of John Nobles dated 23d April 1782--filed 26th Do.
	27th Do	Said Benjn Tutt took Letters of Admon on Estate of said John Nobles as highest Creditor, Dedimus to J. Purves Esqr to qualify appraisers Security Wm. Moore & Jos. Towles. N. B. No farther Proceeding Concerning the above Estate never Returned to this Office
	23d April	Citation to Sarah Bryant on Estate of Robt Bryant filed 26th Do. as Next of Kin-- Letters of Admon granted to Sarah Bryant who qualifyed as Admrix 6 May 1782. Warrant of Appraisemt. Dedimus to John Purvis Esqr to qualify Sarah Bryant as Admrix etc & to qualify appraisers to said Estate-- Admon Bond taken. Securities Benjn. Tutt & David Maxwell--Inventory appraisement & Sale etc. Retured & filled in the ordinary's [office] the 26th of July 1782 and Recorded in page 73 of this Book. ₤ 3296 17 6. Sale ₤ 2296. Cash & paper money ₤ 2479.
	23d April	Citation to Izabel Wallace on Estate of Robt Wallace as Next of Kin--Letters of Admon granted to Izabel Wallace who qualifyed as Admrix--warrant of appraisement. Dedimus to John Purvis Esqr to qualify Izabel Wallace as Admrix etc and to qualify appraisers to said Estate. Admon Bond taken. Securities Benjn Tutt and David Maxwell. The dedimus & Warrant of appraisement Returned, Executed by John Purves, Esqr & filed in this office the 27th of Novr. 1782. Inventory, appraisement and Sale returned to this Office, and Recorded in page 102 of this Book
	26th April	Citation to Frances Brooks on Estate of Elisha Brooks filed 4th May 1782
	4th May	Said Frances Brooks, widow, took Letters of Admon as next of Kin of Estate of Elisha Brooks Deceased. give a Dedimus to John Wyld Esqr to swear appraisers. Admon Bond ₤ 2000 sterling Penalty, Securities John Wyld & John Wallace Augt 3rd Inventory & appraists, filed in the Ordinary's Office ₤ 5542 0 0.

4

Recorded in page 70 of this Book

	26th April	Citation to John Cheney on Estate of James Cheney deceased, filed 3d of May 1782
	3d of May	Said John Cheney & Priceilla Cheney took Letters of Admon as next of Kin, of Estate of James Cheney, deceased. sworn James Thomas, John Grey, Thomas Spraggins & John Turner, appraisers. Admon Bond, Penalty ₺ 2000 sterlg. Securities James Thomas & John Grey.
	3d Do.	I give Letters of Guardianship to John Cheney of Betsey Cheney Minor. Inventory & appraisement filed in the Ordinary's Office the 1st Augt [ ] amount ₺ 1149 5. Recorded [in page 74 of this Book]
7	26th April	James Thomas & William Thomas took a Citation on [Estate] of Danl Thomas deceased

N. B. The Citation never Returned farther proceeding of Said Estate discontinued in this office.

	26th April	Mary Hews took Citation on Estate of William Hews deceased, said Mary Hews dying, her son Joseph Hews took Letters of Admon 23d Decm 1782 on said Estate of Wm. Hews deceased. Warrant of appraisemt. Dedimus to Wm. Kennedy Esqr to qualify appraisers to said Estate. Admon Bond Securities Thos. Brandon & James Noble. 13th February 1783. Inventory & & Appraisement Returnd and filed in the Ordinarys office, amount ₺ 1514 10. also a List or Schedule of 30,000 paper Dollars. ₺ 48750 Recorded in page 47 of this Book.
	26 Do.	Jane Sansom took Citation on Estate of John Sansom deceased as next of Kin.
	Novr. 29th 1782	granted Letters of Admon to Jane Sansom & David Edmingston on Estate of John Sansom who qualifyed as Admon & Admxie. Warrant of appraisemt. myself qualifyed as appraisers David Logan, Alexdr Logan & John Logan. Bond as usual, Securities David Logan & Alexdr Logan. 27th February 1783. Inventory & appraisement Returned & filed in the ordinary's office. ₺ 265 17 6 Recorded in page 62 of this Book.
	26 Do.	Jane Towles took Citation on Estate of Olipher Towles deceased.

N. B. The Citation never Returned, farther proceeding of said Estate discontinued in this Office.

8	26th April	Henry Taylor took Citation on Estate of John Taylor deceased. filed the 12th of July 1782. Said <u>Henney</u> Taylor took Letter of Administration as next of Kin of the estate of John Taylor deceased Administration Bond ₺ 2000 Sterling. Securities Randal Robenson and John Liles, give a Dedimus to George Ruff & Elias Hollensworth Esqrs to Swear appraisers. Mrs. qualified Admix. Octr. 10th the Inventory, apprait. & Sale of Said Estate was filed

        in the Ordinary's Offices & an amount of Book Debts
        due to the Estate
         Recorded in page 100 of this Book

April   Jesse Roundtree took a Citation on Estate of Jethro
      Roundtree, deceased as Next of Kin, 26th Nov. 1782
      granted Letters Admon to Jesse Roundtree, who quali-
      fyed as Admon, warrant of Appraisemt. Dedimus to John
      Murray Esqr to qualify appraisers. Admon Bond
      Securities Daniel Shaw & Simion Cushman.
      30th January 1783 the Inventory & appraisement returned
      and filed in the Ordinary's Office
       Recorded in page 59 of this Book.

1782   Alexander Boyes took a Citation on Estate of Arthur
May 17th Boyes deceased, filed the 29th of May 1782.
29th May Said Alexander Boyes took Letters of Administration
      as Next of Kin, of the Estate of Arthur Boyes
      deceased. Administration Bond ₤ 200 sterling, penalty;
      Col. George Reed and James Seawright, Securities.
      Sworn appraisers, George Reed, John Wilson, Capt.
      John Calhoun & James Seawright.
      Inventory & Appraisement filed the Ordinarys office
      the 26th July 1782. Amount ₤ 508 2 3
       Recorded in pages 71 & 72 of this Book.

May 17th John Wilson and Martha Wilson took a Citation on
      Estate of James Wilson deceased. filed the 29th
      May 1782.
29th May Said John Wilson & Martha Willson, widow, took
      Letters of administration as Next of Kin of the
      estate of James Wilson deceased, administration Bond
      ₤ 2000 sterling, penalty. Securities George Reed &
      John Calhoun. Swore appraisers, George Reed, John
      Calhoun, James Seawright and Alexander Boyes.
      Inventory & Appraisement filed in the ordinary's
      office the 26th July 1782. Amount ₤ 688 2 6
       Recorded in page 101 of this Book.

1782
May 29th Capt. John Calhoun took a Citation on Estate of John
      Calhoun Senr of said District deceased.
      Citation filed in the ordinary's office the 7th of
      October 1782. took Letters of Administration and
      give the Usual Bond ₤ 14,000 (cury.) qualified as
      Admr. granted Warrant of appraisement and a Dedimus
      to Hugh Wardlaw, Esquire to Swear appraisers. Inven-
      tory Returned & filed in Ordinary's office 8th Nov
      1782, and Recorded in page 75 of this Book.

1782   Robert Bond and Abigier Issom took a Citation on the
June 17th Estate of Edward Issom of said District deceased,
      filed the 12th July 1782. Said Abidier Issom as
      Next of Kin & Robt Bond as assistent took Letters of
      Administ. of the estate of Edward Issom deceased.
      Administration Bond ₤ 2000 sterling penalty. Securities
      Aaron Steel, Thos. Harris & Robert Bell; Inventory
      & appraist. filed in the Ordinary's office the 13th
      Septr. 1782.
      Recorded in page 89 of this Book.   ₤ 140 18 3

9 [1782 James Allin took a Citation on the Estate of his
   July 5th] Father Josiah Allin deceased; filed in the Ordinary's
      office the 20th Augt 1782. Said James Allin took

	Letters of Administration on said Estate as Next of Kin. and was qualified as Admin. Give Bond ₺ 14,000 Cury. Surities Enoch Grigsby & Fredk Sisson--got a dedimus directed to William Moore & Solomon Pope to Swear appraisers viz. Wm. Sisson, Enoch Grigsby, Russell Wilson & John Davis. The Inventory & Appraisement filed in the Ordinary's office the 11th of October 1782 and Recorded in page 67 of this Book.
July 11th	John Harvey to a Citation on the Estate of his Brother Thomas Harvey, deceased. Citation filed the 2d August the 5 Agut. took letters of Adminis and qualified as Admin. Give Bond ₺ 14,000 Curreny. Securities Israel Pickens and James Saxon, took a dedimus directed to Col. Hammond & William Jones Esqr. to Swear appraisrs No Inventory, appraisement nor Sale of Said Estate returned to this office
	June 19th 1782. Ann Grasty, widow, took Citation on the Estate of Sharshall Grasty, deceased, filed the 12th. July. Said Ann Grasty took Letters of Administration as Next of Kin, of the Estate of Charchell Grasty deceased, Administration Bond ₺ 2000 Sterling, penalty. Securities Nathl. Spragens and Randol Robeson, give a Dedimus to George Ruff & Elies Hollensworth Esqrs. to Swear appraisers. Inventory & appraisement & Sale filed in the ordinary's office the 10th Octr 1782. Recorded in pages 83 & 84 of this Book.
July 12th	Rebecca George, widow, took a Citation on the estate of David George Deceased, filed 14th Novr 1782. Said Rebecca George & her step-son Wm. George took Letters of Administration warrant of appraisemt., give Bond, Securities James Hogans & David Hutson, give Dedimus to Elias Hollingsworth to qualify appraisers.16th January 1783, the Inventory & appraisement with the list of the Sales of the above's good and Chattels Returnd and filed in the Ordinary's Office, and Recorded in pages 45 & 46 of this Book.
July 22d 1782	The last will & testament of Michael Watson of 96 District dated the 26th May 1782 was probated in the Ordinary's office the 22d of July 1782. by Richman Watson a Subscribing Witness, the other witnesses Robert Stark and Wm. R. Withers. Martha Watson appointed Executorix and Arthur Watson qualifyed an executor, Martha Watson & Robert Stark not qualifyed, a dedimus to Solomon Pope Esqr to qualify Martha Watson Exex, & Robt Stark Exor, and also to qualify appraisers. Martha Watson qualified as an Exex before Solomon Pope Esqr the 27th July
August 22d	Arthur Watson one of the Exers, returned into the Ordinary's office an Inventory & appraisement of the Estate of Michael Watson deceased ₺ 4847 15 0 Give a copy of Said Will to said Arthur Watson, Exr. A list or Schedule of Book accts. & notes of hand due to Said Estate Returned into this office. Recorded in pages 103, 104, 105 & 106 of this Book

1782

July 24th — James McCleskey & Issabella McClesky his wife took a Citation on the Estate of Samuel Paxton deceased as Next of Kin. Citation filed in the Ordinary's Office the 31st of March 1783. the said James McClesky & Issabella McClerksey qualified as an Admin & Admix entered into the usual Bond of ₤ 14,000 Currency. Surities Hugh Baskens and David McClesky Junr. Warrant of appraisement granted, and the appraisers Sworn in the ordinary's office
N. B. No appraisement nor Sale of the above Estate Returned to this office

July 26th — John Rainford took a Citation on the Estate of Edwin Ferned of Horns Creek in said district deceased as highest Creditor.
Augt 3d 1782. Hannah Farned enters a caveat agt. adminer, being granted untill she Can have a hearing. The above Hannah Farned not appering to support her Cavit [sic]. The Citation was filed in the Ordinary's Office the 16th Auguest 1782. Letters of Adminer. was granted to John Rainsford who qualified as Admin. Give Bond ₤ 2000 Sterling. Surities John Herendon and Harmon Galman. Give a Dedimes to LeRoy Hammond & Hugh Middleton to Swear appraisrs. 26th Novr 1782 Inventory & appraisemt. Returned & filed in Ordinary's Office & Recorded in page 79 of this Book

July 30th — Licence Granted & directed to the Revd. John Harris to Solmnize Marriage between Ebenr. Pattigrew and Sarah Stedman, widow, both of 96 District.
The said Ebenr. Pettigrew give Bond ₤ 7000
    Surity John Pettigrew

July 31st — The last Will & Testament of William Golightly of Fair-forest in 96 District, deceased dated the 18th January 1782 was Probated in the Ordinary's Office the 31st July by Moses Foster a Subscribing Witness, the other witnesses Charles James and John Foster. David Golightly Exer. qualified as Such the other Exorx Amey Golightly Not qualified, Letters Testamentory granted & warrant of appraisemt. a dedimus to Henry White and Simon Barwick to qualify appraisers. Inventory & appraisement filed in the Ordinary's Office the 23d of October 1782 (Returned by David Golightly Exr) with an account of Book Debts & Money
    Recorded in pages 84 & 85 of this Book.

Augt 2d — Elisabeth Adams, widow, took Citation on the Estate of James Adams Junr. of Cuffetown, deceased in 96 District as Next of Kin. filed in the Ordinary's Office the 30th August said Elizabeth Adams qualified as Administratrix; took Letters of Administration Give the usual Bond ₤ 14,000 currency. Surities James Harrison and Benjn. Glanton, a Dedimus given to Benjamin Tutt Esqr. to Swear appraisers viz James Harrison, Benjn Glanton, Samuel Anderson and Robert Brayns.
26th Novr 1782 Inventory & appraisemt. Returned & filed in Ordinary's Office.
also a List of the Sale & paper money
    Recorded in pages 68 & 69 of this Book

	1782. Augt 2d	William Dunbar & other Executors of the Estate of George Galphin deceased got New Warrent of Appraisement and a dedimus to qualify appraisers directed to John Murray Esqr. Inventory & appraists. filed in the ordinary's Office the 4th of October 1782. With a list or Inventory of Bonds & Notes due to said Estate etc. Recorded in pages 80, 81, 82 & 83 of this Book.
	Augt. 6th	Harmon Gallman and William Brown of Horns Creek in sd. District took a Citation on the Estate of Joseph Rice of 96 District deceased, as highist Creditors and next of Kin filed in the ordinary's office the 16th Augt. qualified as administrators took Letters of Administration. Give Bond ℔ 2000sterling. Sureties John Rainsford & Casper Galman, a dedimus to William Jones and Le Roy Hammond Esqrs to swear appraisers. Inventory & appraist. filed in the Ordinary's Office the 9th of Octr. 1782. Sale of the Estate & list of Debts. Returned & filed the 28th Decr 1782. and Recorded in page 98 of this Book.
	Augt. 15th	Celia Williams, of Stevens Creek in 96 District, widow took a Citation on the Estate of Charles Williams deceased. Said Citation filed in the ordinary's Office the 23d of August 1782. a Dedimus given directed to John Purvas Esquire to take the usual Bond ℔ 14,000 cury. with two good freehold Surities & qualify Celia Williams Administratrix, and also to Swear appraisers 30th August 1782. the above Dedimus and Bond being duly executed by John Purves Esqr was Returned into the Ordinary's Office & filed, Surities Joshua Gray & Ebenezer Stran. Letters of Administration and Warrent of appraisement granted to the Said Celia Williams Admix 19th Octr 1782. Inventory & appraisement returned & filed in the Ordinary's office Recorded in pages 106 & 107 of this book.
	Augt 15th	John Watson Senr. of Clouds Creek in 96 District took a Citation on the Estate of Charity Anderson deceased as next of Kin. Citation filed in the Ordinary's Office the 17th October 1782. Letters of Admon granted 6th Novr. 1782 to said John Watson. warrant of appraisemt. Dedimus to John Purves to qualify appraisers. Do. to Do. to execute Admon Bond. Securities Edward Court [?] & James Harrison. N. B. Dedimus Returned not Certified to have been Executed. the other papers & proceeding not Returned to this office (except the Bonds) but Said to have been Returned to John Thomas Junr. Esqr. Ordinary's office.
	August 16th	The last Will & Testament of Laurence Rambo of Ninety six deceased, dated the 11th of June AD. 1776 was Probated in the Ordinary's office the 16th August 1782 by John Rainsford, as Subscribing Witness, the other Witnesses John Roebuck & Rebekah Adams; John Herendon one of the Executors qualified as such, the other Exr Laurence Rambo not qualified, Letters Testamentory granted & warrent of appraiset. a dedimus to Le Roy Hammond & Hugh Middleton to Swear appaisers. viz Wm. Jones,

			John Rainsford, Joseph Miller and Thomas Carter. 26th Novr. 1782. Inventory & appraisemt. Returned & filed in Ordinarys Office. And Recorded in pages 98 & 99 of this Book.

12   1782
          Augt. 16th   Jemima Evans, of Beach Island, widow, in Said District took a Citation on the Estate of Richard Evans Deceased as Next of Kin the Citation filed in the Ordinary's office the 20th Septr 1782 to the usual Bond ₤ 14,000. Currency Surities William Jones, Esqr. and Daniel Evans granted Letters of administration and warrant of appraist. a Dedimus to William Jones Esqr. to swear appraisers viz Henry Jones, David Bowers, Adam Hayles & John Sturgengger the said Jemima Evans qualified, as administratrix. 26th Novr 1782, Inventory & appraismt. Returned into the Ordinary's office and Recorded in page 79 of this Book.

          Augt 20th   The last Will and Testament of Burditt Eskridge of Ninetysix District deceased, dated the 23d day of March Anno Domini 1779 was probated in the Ordinary's office the 20th of August 1782 by John Davis a Subscribing witness, the other witnesses Jacob Smith & Sarah Smith, Enoch Grigsby and Jacob Smith qualified as Executors (the Exorx, Nance Eskridge Dead) Letters Testamentory granted and Warrant of appraisement and a Dedimus directed to William Moore & Solomon Pope Esqrs, to Swear appraiser viz. John Davis, Russel Wilson, David Nickelson & Wm. Sisson. 8th Novr 1782 Inventory & appraisemt. Returned & filed in the Ordinary's office.
          Recorded in page 78 of this book also a list of Book accts. etc. in page 92.
          [in margin:] Copy will sent by Russel Wilson, Esqr.

          Augt 22d   Sarah Bowman of Reedy River in 96 District, widow, took Citation on Estate of Jacob Bowman deceased as next of Kin; said Citation filed in the Ordinary's office the 28th of Septr. 1782. granted a Dedimus to Hugh Wardlaw Esqr. to have the usual Bond Executed; and qualified the said Sarah Bowman as Admix. Octr. 2d Said Bond being duly Executed before Mr. Wardlaw with Surities viz Samuel Rosamond & Samuel Wharton free holders in the sum of ₤ 14,000 Currencey being filed in the Ordinary's Office. Letters of Admnr was granted and Warrant of appraisement with a dedimus to Hugh Wardlaw to swear appraisers. 8th Janry 1783. Inventory and appraist. Returned & filed in the Ordinary's office, and Recorded page 39 & 40 of this Book.

          The last will and Testament of James Carter in 96 District, deceased, dated the 9th of November 1779 being carried into North Carolina by the said James Carters widow was probated in North Carolina, Lincoln County, by Thomas Carter and Sarah Carter two of the subscribing witnesses (the other witness Benjn. Johnston) before Robert Alexander & James Johnston Esqrs. by virtue of a dedimus to them directed and dated the 17th of June 1783. The Said Thomas Carter returned the above will into the Ordinary's Office the 22d of

	August 1782, and qualified Executor. the other Executors Littice Mcfarland (Alias Carter) Not qualified, Robert Carter, deceased. give a copy of said wills. August 30th granted Letters Testamentory to Thos Carter and Warrant of appraist. Swore as appraisers Samuel Wimbish, Peter Stertes and Alexander Cla[r]k. Inventory and appraisement filed in the Ordinary's Office the 21st of Septr. 1782. Recorded in page 74 of this Book.
₤ 499 2 6	

[in margin of next three entries:] This part by a Dedimus from John Thomas Junr. Esqr., Ordinary

22d Augt 1785. Letice Mcfarlin formerly the widow Carter, qualified as Executrix.

5th December 1785. Warrant of appraisement granted for the Remainder of the above James Carters Estate appraisers Samuel Winbish, Robert Anderson, Esqr. Geo: Whitefield, Peter Stubes & Alexander Clark.

21st Decr. 1786. The above Warrant of appraisement having been neglected & not taken out of the office, & the appraisers never Sworn. A New Warrant of appraist. is granted, and John Cowan, William Clark, & Alexdr. Clark Sworn appraisers, before me.
Pat: Calhoun, Surrogate.

1787 Jany 6th   Inventory & appraist.
Returned & filed ₤ 616 7 0 Sterling & Recorded page 75 of this book.

13   1782
Augt. 23d   The last Will & Testament of John Hearst of 96 District deceased, dated the 9th of September 1780 was probated in the Ordinary's Office the 23d of Augt 1782 by Robert Erwin a Subscribing witness the other witnesses Charles Teulon & Robert Wilson Mary Hearst Sole Executrix (now Mary Cox) qualified as such. Letters Testamentory granted & Warrent of appraisement. Qualified William Carson, John Bages & Robert Erwin freeholders, as appraisers. 24th Augt give a copy of said will. 23d Novr. 1782 Inventory & appraisemt. Returned & filed in Ordinary's office. together with a Memorandim of Debts due to the Estate, and amount of Notes passed at the vandue Recorded in page 86 of this Book.

24th   The last Will and Testament of James Magill of 96 District deceased, dated 8th of Feby 1779 was probated in the Ordinary's office the 24th of August 1782 by John Johnson a Subscribing witness there other Witnesses George Potts and Cathren Johnson; Anthony Golding Executor qualified as such, the other Executors Robert Cunningham, William Oneal & Henry Oneal not qualified (gon to the British) Letters Testamentory granted, and warrent of appraisement, a dedimus directed to John Wyld & William Moore to qualify Richard Griffen, Anthony Griffen, Richd. Goling [Golding?] & John Johnson, or any three of them as appraisers. (a Copy Will taken 26 Augt.)
8th Novr 1782 Inventory & appraisemt. Returned & Recorded in page 95 of this Book.

	Augt 28	Edeth Coodie of Horns Creek in 96 District took a Citation on the Estate of Arthur Coodie deceased as Next of Kin. filed in the Ordinary's Office the 24th of March 1783. Letters of Administration granted to the said Edeth Coodie who qualified as Administratorix, entred into the usual Bond of ℔ 14,000 cury. Surities Edward Vann & Drury Murfey free-holders. granted Warrant of Appraisement, and a Dedimus directed to Thomas Kee & Aqulea Miles, Esquires or either of them to qualify appraisers. June 23d 1783. Inventory & appraisement Returned & filed. Appraist, Book accts & Notes etc. ℔ 475 9 -.
	28th Novr	Sale of Said Estate Returned ℔ 445 19 6. Do. filed, Recorded pages 43 & 44 of this Book.
	Augt 29th	Michael Harvey of Savannah River in 96 District took a Citation on the Estate of Pinketham Hawkens deceased, as next of Kin (The above Citation lost a New Citation the 6th Septr) filed in the Ordinary's office the 13th September 1782 Letters of Adminr. granted Michl Harvey qualified, Admin, and give the usual Bond ℔ 14,000 Cury. Surities James Christopher and Allen Hinton, granted Warrent of Appraisement and a Dedimus to High Middleton or Thomas Kee to Swear appraisers. 27th Novr 1782 Inventory & appraisemt. Returned etc. into the Ordinary's office in old Currency ℔ 1877 1 6 in Sterling ℔ 266 3 0. Augt 10th 1787. The Sale of the above Estate Returned 180 17 0 3/4 1266 14 - by Michael Harvey difrance of appraist. & Sale 87 5 11 610 7 6 and filed with the other papers in the Ordinarys office with Pat: Calhoun, Surrogate Recorded in page 87 of this Book.
14	1782 Septr. 2d	James Christopher of Cherokee ponds in 96 District took a Citation on the Estate of William Davis deceased, of said District as highest Creditor filed in the Ordinary's office the 13th September 1782. Granted James Christopher Letters of Administration who qualified as Admin. and give the usual Bond ℔ 14,000 cury. Surities Michl. Harvey and Allen Hinton granted Warrent of appraisement and a Dedimus to Hugh Middleton and Thomas Kee to Swear appraisers. 20th Janry, Wart. of appraist. & Dedimus Renewed Inventory & appraist. Returned & filed in the ordinary's office the 28th of March 1783. Recorded paged 44 of this Book.
	Septr 2d	Joachim Bulow of Beach Island in 96 District <u>to</u> a Citation on the Estate of Thomas Appleton of <u>said</u> District as next of <u>Kine</u> filed in the ordinary's office the 13th of September 1782. Letters of Administration granted the sd. Joachim Bulow, who qualified admin. Give the usual Bond of ℔ 14,000 Curecy. Surities David Zubly & William Shinholser. granted Warrent of appraisement, and a dedimus to John Murry and William Dunbar, Esqr to Swear appraisers. 13th Novr 1782. Returned Inventory & Appraisement to be recorded.

Recorded in 68 page of this Book

Do 2d   William Shinholser to a Citation on the Estate of John Shinholser of Beach Island in said District deceased as highest Creditor and Brother to the deceased. filed in the ordinary's office the 13th Septr. 1782. Letters of administration granted to William Shinholser, who qualified admin. give the usual Bond of ₤ 14,000 Currency. Surities David Zubly & Joachim Bulow. granted warrant of appraisement and a dedimus to John Murray & William Dunbar Esqrs. to Swear appraisers. 21st of December 1782. the warrant of appraisemt. renewed;6th Janry 1783 Inventory & appraist. Returned & filed in the Ordinary's office and Recorded page 38 of this Book.

Septr 2d   The last Will & Testament of Christopher Smithers, of Beach Island in 96 District deceased, dated 17th Feby 1781 was Probated in the Ordinary's office the 2d September 1782, by William Shinholser one of the Subscribing witnesses, the other witnesses John Nail and John Tobler; John Sturgenegger Executor qualified as such, the other Executors Catherine Shinholser & Lud Williams Not qualified; granted Letters Testamentory, and Warrant of appraisement, a Dedimus to John Murry & William Dunbar Esqrs. to Swear appraisers. 21st December 1782 the Warrant of appraisement renewed.

Appraisment Recorded in page 60 of this Book.   6th Jany 1782 Inventory and appraisement Returned & filed in the Ordinarys Office. Letters of Guardenship granted to Adam Hiles and John Sturgenegger of George Bender a Minor of 14 or 15 years old, son of George Bender of Beach Island deceased. took Bonds of ₤ 14,000. Sureities Lud Williams, David Bowers & John Clark free Holder.

[Original document lamenated in book between pages 14 and 15:]

Know all Men by These presents that I William Davis of Ninty Six Districk Do promise to pay or Cause to Be paid unto James Christopher or his aras or aSins of the Districk afore Said the full and Just Sum of five hundred pounds South Carolinah Curency on Conditions the Said Davis Do Not or Cannot Make good Sofishent Right to a Sartain track of land lying Between the Chereke ponds Giveing under My hand this 12th day of July 1776   his
                               William X Davis
                                   mark

[reverse side:]

Ninetysix)   So Personally came the within named
District)   James Christopher before me and made
               oath That the within Sum of five hundred pounds currency was the penalty the within named William Davis was bound in to make him lawful titles for the within mentioned land, and that about three months before the date of the within note he paid to said William Davis seventyfive pounds in Specie being the full consideration purchise money, That said Davis is since deceased without making any titles for said land or making any Satisfaction in either part or whole for the same
                                   James Christopher

Sworn to the 2d day of September 1782
before me Pat: Calhoun, JP.

15   1782)
       September)   The last Will and Testament of William Hallum of 96
         6th   )   District, deceased, dated the 9th January 1782, was
                     probated in the ordinary's office the 6th September
                     1782 by Samuel Rosamond, one of the Subscribing wit-
                     nesses, the witnesses Josiah Downen and John Pretter;
                     Jenney Hallum (the widow) Executrix qualified as such.
                     John Hallum Exr. not qualified. granted Letters Test-
                     amentory and Wart. of appraisement, also qualified
                     Samuel Rosamond, James Doblins and James Divlen,
                     Free holders, as appraisers. give also a Copy of
                     said Will. 3d Decr. 1782, Inventory Warrant of Apprai-
                     sement & a list of the division of each Legatees
                     Part sent along. Returned into the Ordinary's office
                     and Recorded in pages 87 & 88 of this Book.

         Septr. 6   Mary Hall, of Enoree in 96 District, Widow, took a
                     Citation on the Estate of James Hall, deceased as
                     Next of Kine, Citation filed and Letters of Admon
                     granted the 8th Novr 1782 to Mary Hall who qualifyed
                     as Admrix on said Estate warrant of Appraisemt. given.
                     Dedimus to Elias Hollingsworth Esqr to qualify apprai-
                     sers. give usual Bond, securities Wm Hall & Thomas
                     Cunningham;23d Novr 1782 Inventory & appraisemt.
                     Returned & filed in Ordinary's office. The sale of
                     said Estate since Returned ℔ 403 6 6 Cury. and a
                     list of Debts paid. Recorded in pages 88 & 89 of
                     this Book.

         Septr 7th   Mary Gibson of Hard labour in 96 District took a
                     Citation on the Estate of Samuel Gibson (late of
                     said District) deceased as next of Kin. said Cita-
                     tion filed in the ordinary's office the 20th Septr
                     1782. Letters of Administration granted the 21st of
                     September to the said Mary Gibson who qualified as
                     Admix, give the usual Bond of ℔ 14,000 Cury. Surities
                     Joseph Dawson & William Carson freeholders. granted
                     Warrant of appraisement and swore appraisers viz
                     Joseph Dawson, William Carson, William Moore. Inven-
                     tory Returned and filed in Ordinary's 11th Novr 1782.
                     An acct. of the sale of said Estate Returned & filed
                     14th Decr 1782.
                     Recorded in page 35 of this Book.

         Septr 7th   William Moore Junr. took a Citation on the Estate of
                     Bazall Bond late of said District deceased as highest
                     Creditor, said Citation filed in the Ordinary's office
                     the 20th of Septr 1782. Do. the 21st Granted letters
                     of Adminr. to the said William Moore who qualified as
                     Admir. and give the Usual Bond of ℔ 14,000 currency
                     Surities Peter Stubes and Robert McAlpin free holders
                     granted Warrant of appraisement and a Dedimus to
                     William Moore, Esqr to Swear appraisers.
                     29th March 1782 granted New Warrent of appraisement
                     N. B. appraisement nor Sale of said Estate returned
                     to this Office, Said to be Returned to John Thomas
                     Junr. Esqr., Ordinary's Office

16   1782
       Septr 9th   Tabitha McKeown of Broad River, widow of George

14

	McKeown, late of 96 District, deceased, Enters a Cavate that no person may obtain Letters of Administration of her said Husbans Estate untill she can have a hearing, as there is a last Will & Testament Probated in the Secretary's Office in Chas. Town where it is Lodged, and has a Copy of said Will Certified from said office. N. B. No farther proceeding of the above had in this office
Septr 11th	Elizabeth Owens, of Norths Creek in Ninetysix District, widow, took a Citation on the Estate of John Owens deceased, of said District as Next of Kin 28th Septr. John Wallace enters a Caveat untill he can have a hearing. N. B. No farther applaycation made nor proceeding had in this office Concerning the above Estate.
Septr 14	Elizabeth Little and James Little in 96 District took a Citation on the Estate of William Little Junr., late of said District deceased as Next of Kin. Said Citation filed in the ordinary's office the 27th of Septr 1782. Letters of Administration to the said Elizabeth Little as Admix and James Little Admin they each qualified as Such and give the usual Bond of ℔ 14,000. Surities John Norris and John McCord free holders. Warrant of appraisement granted. John Norris, John McCord, John Revelin & Andrew Hamilton appointed Appraisers. the same day John Norris & John McCord qualified as appraisers. 23 Novr 1782. Inventory & appraisemt. Returned & filed in Ordinary's Office. Recorded in page 90 of this Book.
Septr 17	Ann Robinson & Moses Chirry of Browns Creek at Broad River in 96 District took a Citation on the Estate of Joseph Robinson late of said District Deceased as Next of Kin, the Citation filed in the Ordinary's office the 13th Feburary 1783. Letters of Adminr. granted to said Ann Robinson (Moses Chirry since Citation granted, deceased) Joshua Palmer and James Bogan entered Securities in the Administration of ℔ 14,000, currency, warrant of Appraisement granted, and a Dedimus to William Kennedy and Samuel McJunkin, Esquires or either of them to qualify said Ann Robinson as Admix, and to execute said Bond, also to Swear Appraisers. N. B. No papers, Nor proceeding Concerning the above Estate Returned to this office Since the above

17

1782 Septr 20th	Richard Barksdale & Patty Sharp (alis Carter) took a Citation on the Estate of Robert Carter late of 96 District deceased as Next of Kin. Septr. 25th Mr. Thomas Carter, Enters a Cavet that no Letters of Adminr. be granted Until he can have a hearing as the deceased Robert Carter left a last Will and Testament.
Septr 23d	Mary Beal of 96 in said District to a Citation on the Estate of Elisha Samuel late of Said District deceased as Next of Kin.

	20th Novr 1782	granted Letters of Admon to Mary Beal, who qualified as Admrix. Warrant of appraisemt. Dedimus to Wm. Moore Esqr to qualify said Mary Beal as Admrix & also to Qualify the appraisers to said Estate. Bond taken with the necessary Securities Viz. Thomas Wilson & James Wilson. The Inventory & appraisement with a list of Debt Returned and filed in the Ordinary's office the 21st Decr 1782. Recorded in page 37 of this Book & page 38.
	Septr 23d Novr. 20th 1782.	Faney Griffin of 96, in said District <u>to</u> a Citation on the estate of James Griffin late of said District deceased as Next of Kin. Letters of Admon granted to Fanny Griffin, who qualifyed as Adrix. Warrant of Appraisemt. Dedimus to Wm. Moore Esqr to qualify said Fanny Griffin as Admrix. also to qualify appraisers to said Estate. Admon Bond, Securities Thomas Wilson & James Wilson. Inventory and appraisement Returned and filed in the Ordinary's office the 13th Decr 1782. and Recorded in page 36 of this Book.
	Septr 23d	Mary Leonard of Little River (Saludy) took a Citation on Estate of Laughlin Leonard late of 96 District Deceased as Next of Kin. Citation filed 8th Novr. 1782 in office. Letters of Admon, Warrant of Appraisemt. Dedimus to John Wyld Esqr to qualify Appraisers. Mary Leonard qualifyed as Admrix. Bond Securities Henry Pearson & James Waldrop all done the 8th Novr 1782. 17th February 1783. Inventory and appraisement of the Estate of Laughlin Leonard deceased Returned and filed in the ordinary's Office. ℔ 2649 3 0. Recorded in page 55 of this Book.
18	1782 Septr 23d	The last will & Testament of James Moore Esqr, late of 96 District Deceased, dated the 12th of January 1782. was probated in the Ordinary's Office of Said District the 23d day of Septr. 1782 before Pat: Calhoun, Surrogate by William Neal one of the Subscribing Witnesses the other Witness William Wilson; William Moore Esqr. one of the Exors therein Named qualified as Such, the other Exers Ann Moor, John Moore & Richard Moore not qualified. a Dedimus directed to John Wylds & Solomon Pope Esquires or either of them to qualify the other Exers, and also to Swear appraisers. Letters Testamentory and warrant of appraisement granted and appraisement Returned & filed in the ordinary's office the 21st December 1782. And Recorded in page 37 of this Book.
	Septr 23d	The last Will & Testament of William Golding late of 96 District Deceased, dated the 4th of September 1777 was Probated in the Ordinary's office of said District the 23d day of Septr 1782. before Pat: Calhoun, Surrogate, by Peggey Golding one of the Subscribing witnesses the other Witnesses James Griffin & Laughlin Leonard. John Golding & Ruben Golding Exers therein named qualified as Such, granted Letters Testamentory and Warrant of Appraisement & a

		Dedimus directed to William Moore & John Wylds Esquires to Swear appraisers. 8th Novr 1782. Inventory & appraisemts. Returned & filed. Recorded in page 85 of this Book.
	Septr 25th	Reuben Beckum of Horns Creek in 96 District took a Citation on the Estate of Demsey Hughes late of said District Deceased as Next of kin. Said Citation filed in the Ordinary's Office the 11th of October 1782. Letters of Administration granted to the said Reuben Beckum who qualified as Admin. Give the usual Bond ℔ 14,000. viz Thomas Beckum & Russel Beckum freeholders. Granted Warrant of appraisement & a Dedimus to Thos. Kees, Esqr. to qualify appraisers. The Inventory & Appraisement Returned & filed in the Ordinary's office the 24th Decr 1782 and Recorded in page 38 of this Book as also a list of the Sales page 38.
	Do 28th	John Green Junr of Enoree in 96 District took a Citation on the Estate of John Green Senr, as next of Kin. No farther proceed in this office of said Estate.
19	1782 Octr 2d	Mary Wood of Lawsons fork in 96 District took a Citation on the Estate of James Woods Esqr late of said District Deceased as Next of Kin. Citation filed 4th Decr 1782, granted Letters of Admon to said Mary Wood. Dedimus directed to Simon Berwick Esqr to qualify her as Admrix take the usual Admon Bond. & dedimus to said S. Berwick Esqr to qualify Appraisers to Estate of said James Wood. Warrant of appraisemt. etc. all done on 10th December Anno Dom 1782. The above Bond Executed and Returned. Surities Martin Armstrong & Joseph Venable Penalty ℔ 14,000 cury. also the Inventory & appraises with a list of accounts of said Estate, filed in the Ordinary's Office the 7th of March 1783.

Appraist ℔ 4472 5 -
Accts Do 5129 6 2
Recorded in page 64 of this Book.

	Octr 2d	Rebecca Woods of Lawsons fork in 96 District took a Citation on the Estate of John Woods late of said District Deceased, as Next of Kin. Citation filed 4th Decr Letters of Admon granted 10 December Anno Dom 1782 to said Rebecca Wood. Dedimus to Simon Ber-
	Appraist. ℔ 697 2 6 Acots 5587 6 Cash 300	wick Esqr to qualify her as Adrix & take the usual Security in Executing the Admon Bond. and a Dedimus to said Simon Berwick to qualify Appraisers to Estate of said John Wood. Warrant of appraisemt. etc. The above Bond Executed & Returned. Surities Martin Armstrong & Joseph Venable penalty ℔ 14,000 cury. also the Inventory & apprait. with a list of accts of said Estate & filed in the Ordinary's office 7th March 1783. Recorded in pages 63 & 64 of this Book.
	Octr 7th	William Hairston to a Citation on the Estate of Thomas Hairston late of 96 District deceased as Next of Kin. 20th Novr 1782 Letters of Admon granted to Wm Hairston who qualifyed as Admon. warrant of

		appraisemt. given. Dedimus to H. Wardlaw Esqr. to qualify Appraisers to said Estate. Admon Bond taken Securities Robt. Maxwell & John McCord. Inventory & appraisement Returned & filed in the Ordinary's Office by Wm. Hairston the 21st of Feburary 1783. ₤ 288 18 11. Recorded in page 50 of this Book.
	Octr 11th	Russell Wilson of Richland Creek in 96 District took a Citation on the Estate of James Butler late of the Same place Deceased, as highest Creditor & Married to the widow of the Deceased. said Citation filed in the Ordinary's Office 30th Octr 1782. Letters of Administration granted to said Russel Wilson 30th Octr 1782 who at same time qualifyed as Admon, give the usual Bond, Securities Viz. Wm. Sisson & James Allen granted warrent of appraisement & Dedimus to Solomon Pope Esqr to qualify Appraisers. 8th Novr 1782. Inventory & appraisemt. Returned to the Ordinary's Office ₤ 103 7 6. 22d Decr 1784 Sale Do. Returned ₤ 125 2 6 Cury. Recorded in page 72 of this Book.
20	1782 Octr 12th	Elcie Hays (between Little River & Bush River) took a Citation on the Estate of Col: Joseph Hays (deceased) as Next of Kin. Citation filed 8th Novr. Letters of Admon granted 8th Novr 1782 to said Alice Hays who qualifyed as Admrix. warrant of appraisement. Dedimus to John Wylds Esqr. Bond Securities, Henry Person & James Waldrop.
	1783 16th January	New Wart. of appraisement granted as the former Wart. of Appraist. was lost also a New Dedimus directed to Robt Gillum & James Mountgomery Esqrs to swear appraisers. 28th Febry 1783. Inventory & Appraisement Returned & filed in the Ordinary's Office. Recorded in page 51 of this Book.
	Do 12th	Elizabeth Tinsley (of Carson Creek) took a Citation on the Estate of Isaac Tinsley late of 96 District deceased as next of Kin. Citation filed 8th Novr 1782 in office. Letters of Admon granted to said Elizabeth Tinsley, who qualifyed as Admrix. Warrant of Appraisement. Dedimus to John Wylds Esqr to qualify appraisers. Bond given . Securities Henry Person, John Richey & Golding Tinsley. Inventory & Appraisement Returned & filed in the Ordinary's office the 17th Febry 1782. ₤ 1443 18 -. Recorded in page 62 of this Book.
	Octr 18th	The last Will and Testament of William Norris late of 96 District Deceased, dated the tenth day February 1781 was duly probated in the Ordinary's Office of Said District the 18th of October 1782 by Howell Johnston one of the Subscribing witnesses, the other witnesses Joseph Abele & Elisabeth Norris; John Fedrick the Exor therein Named qualified as Such. Agness Norris Exex not qualified, a Dedimus directed to Phelimon Waters & Russell Wilson Esqr to qualify the Executrix & Swear appraisers. Letters Testomentory granted and Warrant of Appraisement. Inventory, Warrant of appraisemt. Dedimus to P. Waters. Returned into the Ordinary's 3d Decemr.

1782
Recorded in pages 96 & 97 of this Book

  Do 18th Sarah Lott (Near the Ridge) in 96 District took a
Citation on the Estate of Jesse Lott Deceased as
Next of Kin. filed Citation 3d day of Decemr.
1782, & granted at same time Letters of Admon to
said Sarah Lott, who qualifyed as Admrix, Warrant
of appraisemt. granted. Didimus to Philemon Waters
Esqr. to qualify appraisers. usual Bond & Surities
John Fedrick & James Fedrick.
25th February 1783. Inventory & Appraisement Returned
and filed in the Ordinary's office ₺ 1845 12 6.
Recorded in page 54 of this Book.

21 1782
  Octr 21st Jenney (or Jane) Weaver of Mine Creek in 96 District
took a Citation on the Estate of Aaron Weaver, late
of said District deceased as Next of Kin. Letters
of Admon granted 8th Novr 1782. said Jenney Weaver
qualifyed as Administratrix. Warrant of Appraisemt.
myself qualifyed the appraisers Viz. Russel Wilson,
John Douglas & Lewis Clark. Dedimus to Solomon Pope
to qualify said Jane Weaver as Admrix. Bond Securities, 17th January 1783. Inventory & appraisement
Returned and filed in the Ordinary's office.
               ₺ 590 12 0
Ready Money do 15 Guinas 110 5 -
Recorded in page 63 of this Book.

  30th Octr. granted a Citation to Russel Wilson on Estate of
David Brasswell, deceased, as highest Creditor,
little Saludy. filed Citation & took Letters of
Admon this 8th Novr 1782. Russel Wilson qualifyed
as Admon on said Estate of David Brasswell warrant
of appraisemt. Dedimus to Phelemon Waters to qualify
appraisers. Bond, Securities, Lewis Clark & John
Douglas 17th January 1783. Inventory & appraisement
Returned and filed in the Ordinary's Office.
             ₺ 532 18 6
Recorded in page 40 of this Book.

  30th Octr. granted a Citation to Jude Cobb, widow, of Saludy
River, on Estate of her Husband John Cobbs, deceased,
as Next of Kin, Citation filed in Office, 8th Novr
1782. Letters of Admon Warrant of appraisemt. Dedimus to Hugh Wardlaw to qualify appraisers. Bond Securities Wm Calhoun & Capt John Calhoun, said Jude
Cobbs qualifyed as Administratrix 8th Nov 82.
9th Janry 1783. Inventory & appraisemt. Returned
and filed in the Ordinary's office.
Recorded in page 42 of this Book

  12th Novr Citation granted to Israel Pickens on Estate of
John Williams deceased, as highest Creditor, Citation filed 11th Decemr. 1782 in Ordinary's Office.
same time Letters of Admon granted to said Israel
Pickens on Estate of John Williams. give usual
Admon Bond. Securities William White & Alexdr. Noble
N. B. The Estate had been appraised & sold previous
to grantg. Letters of Admon. 12th March 1783. A
list of the Notes arising from the Sales of Said

19

                        Estate Certified by John Luckie & William White
                        the two appraisers Sworn to in the Ordinary's
                        before Pat: Calhoun, Surrog'te.
                        Recorded in pages 65 & 66 of this Book.

22   1782
            13th Novr   Citation granted to John Towns in right of his wife,
                        she having sent her approbition of ye same, on Est-
                        ate of James Harwick.
            21st Novr 1782. Letters of Admon granted to Jno Towns Junr.,
                        who qualifyed as Admon. Warrant of appraisemt.
                        Dedimus to E. Hollingsworth Esqr to qualify apprai-
                        sers. Bond given Securities. Wm. Wright & Jno Towns
                        Senr. 21st Febry 1782. the Inventory & appraist.
                        with a list of the Sales of said Estate Returned &
                        filed in the Ordinary's Office, amount of appraist.
                                          ₤ 912 8 9
                        amount of Sales Do 780 13 2
                                 Difrance ₤ 231 15 7
                        Recorded in this Book pages 49 & 50

            Novr 15th. Citation to Simeon Cushman on Estate of James Gore,
                        deceased, as next of Kin.
            26th Novr 1782. Letters of Admon granted to said Simeon Cushman
                        who qualifyed as Admon. warrant of appraisemt.
                        given. Dedimus to John Murray Esqr to qualify ap-
                        praisers Admon Bond taken. Securities Daniel Shaw
                        Jesse Roundtree. Inventory & Appraisement Returned
                        & filed in the Office oi Ordinary the 25th of Febry
                        1783. Recorded page 42 of this Book.

            Novr 15th   Marriage License directed to the Revd. Mr. John Har-
                        ris to Solemnize Marriage between Aaron Steel &
                        Elizabeth Cozby, both of Long Cane Settlemt. give
                        Bond, Penalty ₤ 2000 proclamation Money of America,
                        Robt Bond, Security.

            Novr. 8th   The last Will & Testament of John Hogg deceased of
                        Enoree River, of said district of 96, dated the
                        14th of July 1781 was probated in Ordinary's office
                        the 8th Novr. 1782 by William Sparks one of the
                        Subscribing Witnesses, the other Witnesses William
                        Darby, Thomas Wafer. the executors Lewis Hogg &
                        Sarah Hogg. said Lewis Hogg qualifyed as Executor.
                        granted Letters Testamentory. Warrant of appraisemt.
                        & dedimus directed to Elias Hollingsworth to qualify
                        appraisers. 28th January 1783. Inventory & apprai-
                        sement Returned & filed in the Ordinary's office.
                        Recod. page 48 of this Book.

                        The last Will & Testament of William Gordon of
                        Enoree River & of 96 District, dated the 19th of
                        April 1782 by Penelope Perry one of Ye Subscribing
                        witnesses, the other witnesses Wm. Cureton & Thomas
                        Perry. the Exors Elizt. Gordon, Thomas Gordon, &
                        Gabrill Anderson. said Elizabbith Gordon qualifyed
                        as Extrix. granted Letters Testamentory, warrant of
                        appraisemt. Dedimus directed to Elias Hollingsworth
                        Esqr. to qualify appraisers.
                        28th January 1783. Inventory & appraist. with the
                        Sale Returned and filed in the Ordinary's office
                        Record. pages 46 & 47 of this Book.

	1782	[The last Will & Testament of Andw Burney of Beach
23	May 9th	Island, deceased, probated in the Ordinary's Office
	N. B. the	fice 9th of May] 1782 by David Zubly Junr. & Britton
	Wart. of	Dawson and Exer. Britton Dawson & Lud Williams named
	Appraise-	Exors, qualifyed as such. granted at same time Let-
	ment & De-	ters Testamentory. Warrant of appraisemt. Lud
	dimus to	Williams Qualifyed as Exor 26th Novr 1782 at Cuffe-
	John Mur-	town
	ray J. P. to	
	Swear appraisers, is	
	Returned to this Office	
	Not Executed	

N. B. Inventory & Appraisemt. etc. Said to have been returned to John Thomas Junr. Esqr. Ordinary's Office.

1785 May 2d   Lud Williams got a Certificate of his qualifing. as Exects.

1782
Novr 20th   Citation granted to Sarah Johnson and Samuel Otterson on Estate of John Johnson Esqr., deceased, as Next of Kin. 2d December. 1782. Letters of Administration granted to Said Sarah Johnson & Samuel Otterson, who qualified as Admon & Admrix. warrant of Appraisemt. Didimus to Elias Hollingsworth Esqr. to qualify appraisers. Bond taken Securities. Daniel Duff & Chandler Aubrey 28th February 1783. Inventory & Appraisement Returned & filed in the Ordinary's Office.
Recorded in pages 53 & 54 of this Book.

Novr 26th   Citation granted to Rachal Foreman and John Williams on Estate of Jacob Foreman, deceased. Citation filed in the Ordinary's Office, Letters of Administration granted to the Rachal Foreman the 29th January 1783. (John Williams Relinquishing his Claim on the Oath of Isaac Foreman) Mrs. Foreman qualified as Admix. Give the usual Bond of ₤14,000 currency. Surities Isaac Foreman & Benjn Darby. Warrant of Appraisement given and a Dedimus to Thos. Kee & Henry Gendrate Esquires or either of them to Swear appraisers. 28th March 1783. Inventory & appraist. Returned & filed in the Ordinary's Office
Recorded in pages 44 & 45 of this Book.

Novr 23d 82   The last Will & Testament of John Scott Deceased of Savannah River, dated 4th Janry 1780. was probated in Ordinary's Office 23d of Novr 1782 by Samuel Boyd one of the Subscribing witnesses. the other witnesses Jno. Douglass, JOhn Boyd & John Sharpton. the Exors Samuel & James Scott. Samuel Scott qualifyed as Exor 23d Novr 82. granted Letters Testamentory. Warrant of Appraisemt. Dedimus to H. Middleton Esqr. to qualify appraisers. 3d February 1783. the Inventory & appraisment with a list or Schedule Returned & filed in the Ordinary's Office.
Recorded in pages 61 & 62 of this Book.

Novr 23 82   The last will & Testament of Solomon Hencock, deceased, dated the 2d October 1782, was probated in the Ordinary Office 23d of Novr 1782, by Daniel Gorre one of the Subscribing Witnesses, the other

		Witnesses Noah Bonds & Richard Bonds. Execor. John Gorre Senr, who qualifyed as such 23d Novr 1782. granted Letters Testamentory. warrant of appraisemt. Dedimus to George Ruff Esqr to qualify appraisers Inventory & appraist. with the list of Sales of the said Estate Returned by John Bryan & filed in the Ordinary's Office the 6th March 1783 and Recorded in page 52 & 53 of this Book.
24	1782 Novr 22d	[Citation to Ann Moore of] Thicketty Creek, as Next [of Kin, on Estate of Patrick] Moore deceased. N. B. Citation never Returned, no farther proceeding had in this office.
	Novr 30th	William McKinley of Long Cane returned into the Ordinary's office of 96, a Warrant of appraisemt. on Estate of James McKinly deceased, & issue by Wm. Burrows Esqr. the 26th October 1777 etc. same time and Inventory of said Estate to be recorded. Recorded in pages 95 & 96 of this Book.
	Decemr. 4th	Citation to Sally Hampton on Estate of Edward Hampton, deceased, as Next of Kin. N. B. The Citation never Returned, nor no father proceed in this office.
	6th Decr.	The Nuncupative Will of James Foster Made the 4th of May 1782, was probated the 6th day of December 1782 in the Ordinary's Office, by John Cozby, John Foster & Margaret McCarter the Witnesses presents. No father proceeds had in this office of the above Estate
25	1782 Decemr. 12th	Citation to James Brewer on Estate of John Bennit deceased, as next of Kin. Citation filed the 4th January 1783. Letters of Administration granted to the Said James Brewer, who qualified as Admin. too the usual Bond ₤ 14,000 cury. Surities Matthew Devori & Bryan Green free holders. granted Warrant of Appraisement. and a Dedimus to Henry Gindrat & Thomas Kee, Esqrs. to Swear Appraisers. Inventory & appraisement with the Sale of Said Estate Returned and filed in the Office of Ordinary the 29th of March 1783. appraist. ₤ 155 5 Recorded page 41 of this Book.
	Decemr. 13th	Citation to William Griffin on Estate of John Griffin, deceased, as Next of Kin. No farther proceed in this office.
	Decr 13th	The last will & testament of John Montgomery, deceased, was probated in the Ordinarys Office by Samuel Finley one of the Subscribing Witnesses. Letters Testamentary given. said James Finley qualifyed as Exor. 6th March 1783 part of the Inventory & appraisement of the Estate of Said John Montgomery Returned by said James Finely Exr, filed in the ordinary's office, the other of said Inventory & appraist. Destroyed when Samuel Finley's house was Burned by the Enemy. 12th March 1783. A list of the Sales of Said Estate Returned & filed

		in the Ordinary's Office. Recorded in pages 55 & 56 of this Book & page 57.
	Decemr. 23d	Citation to Elizabeth Hews of Long Cane on Estate of John Hews deceased, as Next of Kin. Citation filed in the Ordinary's Office the 29th of February 1783. Letters of Administration granted to the Elizabeth Hews, who qualified as Administratrix Entered into the usual Bond of ₤ 14,000 curreny. with two Free-hold Surities viz Joseph Abel & Moses Braford. granted Warrent of Appraisement and Swore appraisers in the Ordinary's Office 28th March 1783. Inventory and Appraisement with the Sale of Said Estate Returned, and filed in the Ordinary's Office. Recorded in page 53 of this Book.
26	1782 Decr 24th	Citation Granted to William Anderson of Reedy River on the Estate of Peter Wood of Reaburns Creek, deceased as highest Creditor. Not proceed farther in this Office of Said Estate.
	1783 Jany 3	Citation to William Caldwell of Mud lick on Estate of John Caldwell Esqr Deceased, as Next of Kin. January 14th the Citation filed in the Ordinary's Office and granted letters of Administration to William Caldwell & James Caldwell with a Dedimus to Robert Gillum Esqr to take the usual Bond of ₤ 14,000 Currency with two good free holder Surities
	Appraist. ₤ 2309 12 6 Sales Do ₤ 2861 15 -	and to Administer the usual Oath to them as Admins and to Swear the Appraiser. The above Bond being duly Executed the 21st of Jany 1783. And William Caldwell & James Caldwell qualified as Administrators. Surities entred in Said Bond, Richard Griffin & Bartlitt Saterwhite. The Inventory & Appraisement of Said Estate, with a list of the Sales was Returned by Wm. Caldwell & filed in the Ordinary's Office the 17th of March 1783. and Recorded in pages 42 & 43 of this Book.
	Jany 8th	Citation to Henry King of Little Saludy on Estate of Giles Burdit Deceased, as having Married Averilla the widow of the deceased who has sent her approbation of the same. February 1st 1783. filed the Citation in the Ordinary's Office and Granted Letters of Administration to the Said Henry King, who qualified as Admin, entred into the Usual Bond of ₤14,000 Currency. Surities Wright Nicholson and Michael Deloach, granted Warrant of appraisement and a Dedimus to Solomon Pope Esqr. to Swear appraisers. 13th March 1783. Inventory & appraisement with a list of the Sales of Said Estate Returned & filed in the Ordinary's Office. Recorded in page 41 of this Book.
	Jany 11th	Citation to Sarah Ford of Indian Creek on the Estate of Bolden Ford, deceased, as Next of Kin; 28th January 1783. filed in Ordinary's Office. granted a dedimus to William Farr and Elias Hollensworth Esquires or either of them, to have the Usual Bond (given by Admins. of ₤14,000 currency) Executed Surities Able Anderson & Francis Strother, also to

		qualify Sarah Ford as Admix and Swear appraisers then to Deliver the Letters of Administration dated this day, to wit the 28th day of January 1783. N. B. The above papers & proceedings are not returned to this office (but supposed to be Returned to John Thomas Junr. Esqr, Ordinary's Office)
27	1783 Jany 13	Thomas [Murphey of Duncans Creek took a Citation] on the Estate of Joseph Grear of Mud-Lick deceased as highest Creditor & Next of Kin. 12th March 1783 Citation filed in the Ordinary's Office, granted Letters of Administration to the said Thomas Murphey who qualified as Administrator. entred into the usual Bond of ₤14,000 currency. Surities Robert Neal, Isaac Mathews and Benjn Killgore Esqr. granted Warrant of appraisement and a Dedimus directed to Benjn Killgore Esqr to Swear appraisers. No farther proceed in this Office Concerning the above Estate.
	Do 13th	Benjamin Kilgore Esqr of Duncans Creek took a Citation on Estate of Patrick McDavid deceased, as highest Creditor & at the request of the deceased's widow Roseana McDavid. 28th March 1783. Citation filed in the Ordinary's Office, granted Letters of Administration to the Said Benjn Killgore who qualified as Administrator Entred into the usual Bond of ₤ 14,000 Currency. Surities George Berrey & William Fowler, granted Warrant of appraisement, and a Dedimus directed to James Montgomery Esqr to Swear appraisers. & Return the same in the time prescribed by Law. N. B. No appraisement nor Sale etc. of Said Estate returned to this office but said to have been Returned to John Thomas Junr Esqrs. Ordinary's Office.
	Do 14th	Citation granted to Samuel Strain on Estate of James Strain late of Long Cane Settlement deceased as Next of Kin. filed in the Ordinary's Office the 25th of January. Letters of Administration granted to the Said Samuel Strain who quallified as Admin took the usual Bond of ₤ 14,000. Surities John Strain & David Strain and give Warrant of Appraisement. N. B. No Inventy. appraist. nor Sale of the above Estate Returned to this Office.
28		A Citation granted by John [Ewing] Calhoun to Abraham Richardson as highest Creditor on Estate of James Ray of 96 District dated the 28th December 1782. filed in the Ordinary's Office, the 20th January 1783. Letters of Administration granted to the said Abraham Richardson as highest Creditor who qualified as Admin. give the usual Bond of ₤ 14,000 currency. Warrant of appraisement granted & a dedimus to Thomas Kee Esqr. to Swear appraisers. 28th March 1783. Inventory & appraist. Returned Recorded in page 59 of this Book.
		28th Decr 1782 Citation granted by John Ewing Calhoun to Joshua Hammond on Estate of John Hammond Senr deceased as Next of Kin, with Letters of

	Admin to be granted with the will Annexed, filed in the Ordinary's Office the 20th January 1783. having his Mother's Ann Hammonds approbation a dedimes granted to Thomas Kee Esqr to probate the said last will & Testament of John Hammond by Swearing the Subscribing Witnesses & to Certify the Same under his hand & Seal No Return since made into this office.
Janry 28 1783	William Prat took Letters of License (directed to the Revd. John Harris) To Solemnize Marriage between the Said Wm. Prat & Mary Drennan, Spinster, both of Long Cane Settlement in 96 District, give Bond penalty ₺2000 proclamation Money of America, Surity William Drennan.
Feby 4th 1783	The last Will & Testament of James Crawford Senr, late of Long Canes in 96 District deceased, dated 7th Novr AD 1780 was probated in the Ordinary's Office the 4th of February 1783 by William Alexander one of the Subscribing Witnesses the other Witnesses John Sprott, and John Cochran, Joseph Turnbull one of the Executors named in said Will qualified as Such and took Letters Testamentory (the other Exor Jesse Campble not qualified having Gon off with the British) No Returns Since to this made.
Febry 13th 1783	The last Will & Testament of Richard Hughs late of 96 District deceased, dated the 5th of April 1781 was probated in the Ordinary's Office the 13th of February 1783 by James Bogan one of the Subscribing Witnesses, the other Witnesses John Allbritton, Jeptha Hollensworth and James Johnston; Joshua Palmer & James Bogan Named Executors in Said Will qualified as Such. and took Letters Testamentory, Warrant of Appraisement and a Dedimus directed to William Kennedy & Samuel McJunkin Esquires, to Swear appraisers. No return since made to this office.
1783. Febry 13th	A Citation granted to Mary Mayfield on the Estate of John Mayfield late of Brown's Creek in 96 District Deceased, as next of Kin. N. B. The Citation never Returned, no farther proceedings had of said Estate in this Office.
Febry 24th 1783	The last Will & Testament of Thomas Pickett late of 96 District deceased, dated the 26th of May 1782 was probated in the Ordinary's Office the 24th of February 1783 by William Goode the other Witness Thos Runnolds. Mille Pickett one of the Executors named in said Will qualified as Exex, the other Exor William Runnolds not qualified. Letters Testamentory granted to the said Mille Pickett, with warrant of appraisement, and a dedimus to Thomas Kee Esqr to qualify appraisers. No Inventory, appraist. nor Sale of the above Estate Returned to this Office.
Febry 27th	A Citation granted to Richard Corley on the Estate

		of James Grigsbey late of little Saludy in 96 District Deceased as highest Creditor, and now Married to Millenr Grigsbey widow of the said Deceased. 13th March 1783. Citation filed in the Ordinary's Office, said Richd. Took Letters of Administration in right of his Wife she having sent her approbation of the Same. the Said Richard Corley qualified as Administrator, entred into the usual Bond of ₤14,000 Currency. Surities Bartelet Bledsoe and David Nichelson. granted Warrant of appraist. and a Dedimus to Solomon Pope Esqr. to qualify appraisers. No farther Returns made of said Estate to this office.
	Feby 28th	Mark Love to a Citation on the Estate of William Orr, late of Tagger [Tyger] River in 96 District deceased, as Next of Kin. 15th March 1783. Citation filed in the Ordinary's Office, the said Mark Love qualified as Administrator. entred into the usual Bond of ₤14,000. Currency. Surities Andrew Ross & James Caldwell Senr. Letters of Administration granted and Warrent of appraisement with a Dedimus to Elias Hollingsworth and Col. Thomas Brandon, Esqrs to qualify appraisers. N. B. No Return Concerning the above Estate made into this Office Since the above.
30	1783 March 12th	Thomas Farrow of Enoree in 96 District took a Citation on the Estate of William Berrey late of said District Deceased, as Highest Creditor. March 28th 1783. George Berrey as Eldest son of the deceased enters a Cavete against letters of Administration being granted untill he can have a hearing. N. B. No farther Proceedings the parties NOt applayint this Office
	Do 12th	Milley Letcher of Stevens Creek in 96 District took a Citation on the Estate of James Letcher late of Said District Deceased, as Next of Kin. 24th March 1783. the above Citation filed in the Ordinary's Office. The Said Milley Letcher qualified as Administratorix entered into the usual Bond of ₤14,000 currency with two freehold Securities viz William Carson & Benjn Blackey. Granted Letters of Administration and Warrant of Appraisement also a Dedimus directed to John Purvas & Thomas Kee, Esquires or either of them to qualify appraisers. N. B. No appraisement nor Sale of Said Estate Returned into this office.
	March 18th	William Thomas Caldwell took Letters of License directed to the Revd. John Harris to Solemnize Marriage between the said Wm. T. Caldwell and Elisebath Williams Spenster both of 96 District, give Bond of ₤2000 penalty Proclamation money of America Surity Alexdr. Noble.
	March 19th	Baveley Cox & William Cannon of Warriers Creek in 96 District to a Citation on the Estate of William Cox late of said District Deceased as Next of Kin No proceeding farther had in this office of said

		Estate.
	March 19th	William Simpson & Margaret Simpson his wife, of Cane Settlement in 96 District to a Citation on the Estate of Samuel Mann late of Said District Deceased as Next of Kin. 31st March 1783. Said Citation filed in the office of Ordinary, the said William Simpson qualified as Admin. and said Margerat Simpson qualified as Admix, they entered into into the usual Bond of ₺14,000 Currency. Surities Francis Sutherland and William Manson; granted Letters of Administration, and Warrant of appraisement. also qualified William Luckie, Francis Sutherland & William Manson as Appraisers. The Inventory & appraisement said to have been Returned to the Ordinarys office at John Thomas Junr. Ordinary's Office.
31	1783 March 24th	The last Will & Testament of Robert Melvill late of 96 District Deceased dated the 12th of Septr 1782 was probated in the Ordinary's Office the 24th day of March 1783 by Nicolas Maxwell one of the Subscribing witnesses, the other Witness William Maxwell; Robert Maxwell one of the Executors named in the said last will & Testament, qualified as Executor, the other Mary Melvill Executrix and John Maxwell not qualified. Letters Testamentory granted to the said Robert Maxwell without Warrent of appraisement as the said Testator having Willed and Bequeathed his whole Estate by Legacies to the several Legaties therein Named, and as specified The said Robt. Maxwell acting Exor to return into the Ordinary's Office of said District (within the time prescribed by Law) a just & true Inventory together with a list of Schedule of the Book accounts of said Testator. 25th June 1783. an Inventory together with a list of Schedule of debts due to said Estate was Returned by sd. Robt Maxwell & filed in the office. and Recorded in pages 57 & 58 of this book.
	March 25th	Elisabeth Marble Smith & Francis Jones of Saludy in 96 District took a Citation on the Estate of Smallwood Smith, late of said District Deceased as Next of Kin. N. B. The Citation never Returned no farther proceeding Concerning the above Estate in this office.
	March 31st	Hugh Middleton of Savannah River in 96 District took a Citation on Estate of William Kindel deceased as highest Creditor. N. B. Citation not returned no farther proceed in this Office.
	1786 Septr 25th	John Sharp & Patty his wife took a Citation (from John Thomas Esqr, Ordinary of 96 District)on the Estate of Robert Carter, late of said District, Deceased, as Next of Kin. The Same Certified by the Revd. Robert Mecklen was Read & published after divine Service 27th of Septr 1786. The Kindred & Creditors to appear before Patrick Calhoun Esqr. on the third Saterday in October then Next to Show Cause if any they have Why the said Administration should not be granted.

October 21   The Said Citation being Returned to me as directed
and no person appearing to make any objection nor
no Will produced nor known of in being, upon Oath
the said John Sharp & Patty his wife qualified.
John Sharp as Admin & his wife Patty As Admix, of
the Same & entred into the usual Bond of ₺2000
Current money of South Carolina. Securities Joseph
Calhoun and George Crasswell, freeholders. where-
upon by Virtue of a Dedimus from the sd. John Thomas
Esqr, Ordinary, dated the 25th of Septr 1786 and to
me directed for that purpose did grant & give to
the said John Sharp & Patty his wife (as Next of Kin
to the said Deceased) Letters of Administration and
Warrant of Appraisement, also qualified William
Clark, Joseph Colhoun, George Crasswell & Robert
Patterson (free-holders) Appraisers.
Certified this 21st day of October AD 1786 at Long
Canes in 96 District.   Pat: Calhoun Surrogate
N. B. the whole proceeding to be returned to John
Thomas Esqr, Ordinary to be recorded.

[pages 32 and 33 are blank]

34   Mary Gibson   Crockery Ware   1 - -

35   South Carolina   )
Ninety Six Distt.   ) Inventory and appraisement of the Estate of
Samuel Gibson of the Sd. District deceased taken the 2nd day of
Novemr. 1782 by Joseph Dawson, William Moore, and William Carson
Sworn appraisers. Includes Negroes Peter, Singaric, Clark & Frank.
Total appraisement in old currency ₺ 1401 2 0. 1124 Contenental
Dollars 1826 10 -. Examined & Certified by Pat: Calhoun Surrogate.

35-6   An Account of the Sales of the above Estate of the Sd. Saml Gibson
deced. sold by Mary Gibson Adminrx. the 12th Decemr 1782. Purchasers:
Mary Gibson, Thoms. Carson, John Hearst, Samuel Bell.
Examined & Certified by Pat: Calhoun Surrogate.

36   An Inventory and Appraismt. of the Estate of James Griffitt deceased
made the 30th Novr 1782. Sworn appraiser. Thomas Wilson, Mathew Mc-
Millin & Ruben Halloway. Total in old Curency ₺ 166 18 9. Examined &
Certified by Pat: Calhoun Surrogate.

36-7   An Inventory and Appraisement of the Estate James Norrel deceased dated
the 14 of Octr. 1782 by William Agny, Ricd. Allison and William Hagewood. Includes Negroes Dick, Charty. Total appraisement in old currency
₺1642 10 -. Examined & Certified by Pat: Calhoun Surrogate.

37   An Inventory and Appraisement of the Estate of James Moore Esqr. of 96
deceased made the 16 Novemr 1782 by the Appraisers Mathew McMillen,
William Mathew, and John Jackson. Includes Negroes Jack, Little Jack,
Acon, Kitt and Charles; Silva her children Haner, Sarah, Pery, Edmond
& Phels; Patience & Children Lidy & Meriot; Tamer and children Edy,
Joe & Allen; Lucy, Pindar, Patty and Bob; Sillas, Doll, and Stepney;
400 lb cotton, Parcel of Tobacco. ₺ 8782 15 -. Examined & Certified by
Pat: Calhoun Surrogate.

37-8   An Inventory and Appraisment of the Estate of Elisha Samuels deced made
the 30th Novemr 1782 by Thomas wilson, William Hoggwood and Mathew Mc-
Millan appraisers. Includes negroes (not named). Book accounts include 1775
William Brown; Decemr 1776 John Ekins, Champ Terry; April 24 1776 Gabriel
Smothers; May 18 John Grisset; May 22 Charles Herd, Edward Wilkisson;

March 13th 1776 Beverly Barksdale, William Neal, William Tyner, Jacob Martin, Majr. Champ Terry, Henry Liveley.[No total of inventory given] Examined & Certified by Pat: Calhoun, Surrogate.

38 An Inventory and Appraisment of the Estate of Demsey Hughs, deceased, made the 9th of Novr. 1782 by the appraisers Thomas Beckum, Michael Buckhalter & John Pursel. Includes one negro man (not named). Total appraisement ℔ 674 15 0. Examined & Certified by Pat: Calhoun, Surrogate

1782 An account of the Sales of the Estate of the above Demsey Hughs, as sold by Reuben Beckum Admir of the Same. Buyers: Mrs. Hughs, Reuben Beckum bought 1 Negro Peter. Total in Old Currency ℔ 708 15 0. Examined & Certified by Pat: Calhoun Surrogate.

An Inventory and Appraisement of the Estate of John Shinholser, deceased Made the 30th of December 1782 by John Sturzenneger, John Tobler & Adam Hill. Includes one negro (not named). Total in old Currency ℔ 478 2 6. N. B. No Sale Returned. Examined & Certified by Pat: Calhoun Surrogate.

39 1782. An Inventory and Appraisement of the Estate of Jacob Bowman, Intestate, made the 26th of Octr and 20th of Novr last past by the appraisers to wit Ebenezer Starns, John Hugs & Duke Pinson, as shewen to them by Sarah Bowman Admixr. Includes Negroes: Nell, Dave, Mill, Jane and Tupter, Wine. Total in old Currency ℔ 2960 4 6. Examined & Certified by Pat: Calhoun, Surrogate.

39-40 A list of Scheduel of Book Accounts of Said Jacob Bowman's Estate. Names: John Caldwell, John Willard, Robert & Henry Jones, Fredrick Felts, Martin Willard, John Brown, Thomas Wood, Robert Hinton, Joseph Williams, James Philpote, Jacob Wright, William Anderson, Laughlin Maddin, Thomas Carter, Barnney Kiles, Mr. McLine, Joseph Jefferson, Sarah Wright, John Parker, Sherwood Allen, Benjamin Hodge, Benjamin Brown, Lewis Benton, Joseph Box, Thomas Allison, Docter Warren, Charles Broadaway, Joseph Adkins, Hugh Brown. ℔ 242 13 7. Examined & Certified by Pat: Calhoun Surrogate. N. B. No amot of Sales sent to this office.

40 An Inventory & Appraisement of the Estate of David Brasswell, Intestate, made the 22d of Novr 1782 by the appraisers Andrew Lee, Levi Manning, & Thomas Gibson. (Russell Wilson, Admir. Includes Negro Jeff. Total in old Currency ℔ 532 18 6. N. B. No Sales Returned to this office. Examined & Certified by Pat: Calhoun, Surrogate.

41 An Inventory and appraisement of the Estate of Giles Burditt, Intestate, (Henry King, admir.) made the 25th of February 1783 by the Appraisers to wit, Wright Nicholson, Michael Delouch, and Jesse Ternigin, appraisers. Total ℔ 39 3 7.
An Inventory of the Sales of Said Estate Made the 25th of Feby 1783. Sold by Henry King, Admir. Purchasers: Henry King, Michl Delouch, Jesse Ternigin, George Mason. Amount of Sales & Note ℔ 119 15 11. Examined & Certified by Pat: Calhoun, Surrogate.

An Inventory & Appraisement of the Estate of John Bennit Intestate (James Brewer, Admir) made the 14th of January 1783 by the appraisers John Kitt, Briant Green & Johannes Blacklard (the last is a Duch name). Total ℔ 155 5 0.
An account or list of the Sales of Said Estate by James Brewer Admir. (no date but prior to the 29th of March 1783). Total ℔ 156 3 9. Examined & Certified by Pat: Calhoun, Surrogate.

	1783
42	An Inventory & Appraisement of the Estate of John Cobb (Intestate) made the first day of January 1783 by Isaac Mitchall, Benjamin Mitchall & George Heard, appraisers, as was Shewn to them by Jude Cobb, Admrx. of the Same. Total appraisement ₤ 236 10 0. Examined & Certified by Pat: Calhoun, Surrogate N. B. No return of Sale made to this office.
	An Inventory & Appraisement of the goods & Chattels of James Cone, Intestate, made the 6th day of January 1783 by Jesse Rowntree, Nathl Bacon & Vachal Davis Appraisers as was shews to them by Simon Cushman, Admir. Total ₤ 138 - -. Examined & Certified by Pat: Calhoun, Surrogate. N. B. no return of Sale made to this office.
42-3	An Inventory & appraisement of the Estate of John Caldwell Esqr, Intestate, made the 21st of January 1783 by Bartlitt Saterwhite, Richard Griffin & Daniel Megin, appraisers. William Caldwell & James Caldwell, Admrs. Includes Negroes Leander, Granville, Tom, Dick. Total appraisement ₤ 2309 12 6. Examined & Certified by Pat: Calhoun, Surrogate.
	An Account of the Sale of Said Estate, the fifth of February 1783, by William Caldwell & James Caldwell Administrators; William Caldwell, James Caldwell, John Caldwell, David Caldwell, John Richey, Richard Griffin, purchasers. Total ₤ 2861 15 -. Examined & Certified by Pat: Calhoun, Surrogate.
43-4	An Inventory & Appraisement of the Estate of Arthur Coodie, Intestate, made the 21st of April 1783 by Lilleston Pardue, Drury Murfey, & Edward Vann, appraisers, Edeth Coodie, Adminx. Includes Negroes Jude, Toney, Coggo, Jene, January, Sam. Total amount ₤ 477 17 6, sterling. Book accounts, notes in old Currency ₤ 460 16 11. Examined & Certified by Pat: Calhoun, Surrogate.
	An Account of the Sale of the above Estate the 15th of March 1784 by Edeth Coodie Adminx, and Certified by James King, Cryer of the vandue. Purchasers not listed. Examined & Certified by Pat: Calhoun, Surrogate.
44	An Inventory & Appraisement of the Estate of William Davis, of Ninety Six District, Intestate, made the 20th of March 1783, by William Covington, Alen Hinton and John Currey, Sworn appraisers, James Christopher admir. Includes tracts of land 75 acres, 100 acres, 200 acres, 150 acres. Total ₤ 421 10 --. [In margin:] N. B. No Right to appraise Lands. No Acc. of Sales Returned to this office of the above Estate. Examined & Certified by Pat: Calhoun, Surrogate.
44-5	An Inventory & Appraisement of the Estate of Jacob Foreman, of Ninety Six District, Intestate, made the 24th of March 1783 by Isaac Foreman, Samuel Walker and Lecon Ryen, Sworn appraisers. Rachiel Foreman, Adminx. Total ₤ 1001 5 3, old Currency. Also a note of hand for Six likely Negroes. Total notes of hand ₤ 525. N. B. No acct. of any Sale of Said Estate sent to this Office. Examined & Certified by Pat: Calhoun, Surrogate.
45	An Inventory & Appraisement of the Estate of David George of Ninety Six, Intestate, made the 22d of November 1782 by John Gormon, George Ashford & William Hill, sworn appraisers, Rebecca George Adminx, William George Adminr. Includes Negroes Eseks, Loos, Peter, Sam & Ned. Total in old currency ₤ 1904 11 0. Examined & Certified by Pat: Calhoun, Surrogate.
45-6	An account of the Sales of the Said Estate as Returned by Rebecca George, Adminx & William George Admin of the Same, dated Decr. 12th 1782. Purchasers not listed. Total ₤ 1743 10 6.

	An Inventory & appraisement of the Estate of William Gordon, Testator, Deceased, made the 27th of Decr. 1782 by William Hamilton, George Gordon & James Caldwell, sworn appraisers, Elisabeth Gordon Exerx. Includes Negroes: Venus, Sam, Bob. Total ₺ 1587 15 0. The amount of the Notes due to the Estate ₺ 776 15. Examined & Certified by Pat: Calhoun, Surrogate.
46-7	The Sales of the Estate of the Said William Gordon, Deceased as Sold at Public Vandue January 15th 1783. Purchasers: Elish. Gordon, Willm. Gordon, Menis Liles, Eg Virden, Rebekah Anderson, John Clark. Total ₺ 1825 5 6.
47	An Inventory & appraisement of the Estate of William Hughs, Intestate, made the 4th of January 1783 by Thos Brandon, Willm Farr & Charles Sims, Sworn appraisers. Joseph Hughs, Admin. Includes 4 negroes (not named). Total ₺ 1514 10. Includes a Book Debt to Moses Cherrey. For Thirty Thousand Paper Dollars ₺ 48750. Examined & Certified by Pat: Calhoun, Surrogate. N. B. No acct. of Sales Returned to this Office.
	An Inventory & appraisement of the Estate of Jesse Lott of Ninety Six District, Intestate, made the 11th day of January 1783 by James Fredrick, Hawell Johnson, & John Fredrick, sworn appraisers. Sarah Lott, Adminx. Continued Over to page 54. [above entry stricken]
48	An Inventory and appraisement of the Estate of John Hogg, Deceased, Testator, made the 27th of Decr 1782 by Robert Rutherford, William Dawkins, and Daniel Johnson, sworn appraisers (Lewis Hogg acting Exr.) Total ₺ 1303 12 6. Examined & Certified by Pat: Calhoun, Surrogate.
	Of Bonds, Notes & Book Accts. 1 Note on James & Samuel Lindsey due 19th July 1780 1 Note on Wm. Handcock & Wm. Cureton due 19th July 1780 1 Note on Wm Cureton & Nathl. Davis due 19th July 1780 1 Note on Wm Green Deceasd. due 19 July 1780 1 Bond on Thos. Gordon Due 27 Augt. 1778 1 Note on Wm Cureton Due 20 Aprl 1780 1 Note on Wm. Handcock Due 27 May 1780 1 Note of Jams. Killy & Wm Wadlington Due 19 July 1780 1 Note on John Towns in gold or Silver Due 1st July 1781 To a Book Acct. against Wm. Chandler in gold or Silver To a Book Acct. against Wm. Cureton from Janr. 10th to Aprl 1780 To a Book Acct against Wm Wadlington. amount of dollars 1783 @ 32/6 is ₺ 2903 12 6 Examined & Certified by Pat: Calhoun, Surrogate
49	An Inventory & appraisement of the Estate of James Harwick, Intestate, made the first day of December 1782 by Thos. Smith, Joseph Franklin, Daniel McKay & John Gormon, sworn appraisers. John Towns, Junr. admir. Includes Negroes (not named). Total amount ₺ 912 8 9.
49-50	A list of the Sales of the above Estate dated the 24th of December 1782. Purchasers not listed. Examined & certified by Pat: Calhoun, Surrogate
50	An Inventory & Appraisement of the Estate of Thomas Hariston, Intestate, made the 18th day of December 1782 by John Irwin, John Calhoun, and Samuel McMurtrie, sworn appraisers, William Hairston, Admin. Total ₺ 288 18 11. Examined & Certified by Pat: Calhoun, Surrogate. N. B. Sale of Said Estate return to this office.

| 51 | An Inventory & Appraisment of the Estate of Joseph Hays, Esqr, Intestate, made the 31st of January 1783 by Thos. Johnston, James Smith, & James Goggens, sworn Appraisers, Alcie Hays, Admirx. Includes Negroes Julis, Prince, and 3 not named. Total in old currency ₺ 1889 12 6.
N. B. No acct. of Sale Returned to this Office.
Examined & Certified by Pat: Calhoun, Surrogate. |
|---|---|
| 51-2 | An Inventory & Appraisement of the Estate of Solomon Hencoch, Testator, Deceased, made the 29th of Novr. 1782 by Daniel Goore, Willimson Liles, & Richard Bonds, sworn appraisers, John Gorre Senr. Exer. Includes Legesees given to Wm Hencock, 1 Negro boy named Harry, half a Negro boy Isaac.
Legesees given to Richard Handcock, 1 Negro fellow Jack, half a Negro boy Isaac
Legesees to Sarah Hancock, 1 Negro wench Tamer, 1 Negro Girl Tab, 1 Negro boy Jo;
Legesees lent to Ann Hill, 1 negro wench Sarah.
Total in old Currency ₺ 2592 13 0.
Examined & Certified by Pat: Calhoun, Surrogate. |
| 52-3 | An Account of the Sales of the above Estate, of Solomon Hencock. dated the 4th of January 1783. Purchasers: Richard Hencock, Sarah Hencock, Wm. HanDock. Total ₺ 254 15 6.
Examined & Certified by Pat: Calhoun, Surrogate. |
| 53 | An Inventory & appraisement of the Estate of John Hewes, Intestate, made the 10th of March 1783 by John Young, Moses Brawford, & Joseph Abel, sworn appraisers. Elisabeth Hewes, Admirx. Accounts include Andrew Ross, James Mefaron & John Cox, Robart McClinton, William Tork; ₺ 12 10 shilings due from the Estate of Joseph Akins deceased.

Account of the Sales of Said Estate the 20th of March 1783. Purchasers: James Patterson, Rachal Cohran, James Mcfaron, Elizebeth Hewes. Amount in old Currency ₺ 27 18 6.
Examined & Certified by Pat: Calhoun, Surrogate. |
| 53-4 | An Inventory & Appraisement of the Estate of John Johnston, Esqr, Intestate, late of 96 District made the 3d day of January 1783 by William Murray, Thos. Gordon and Thos Brandon, sworn appraisers. Sarah Johnston Admirx, Samuel Otterson Admir of the Same. Includes Negroes (not named). Total ₺ 1731 10 0 in old currrency.
Examined & Certified by Pat: Calhoun, Surrogate.
N. B. No Sales of Said Estate returned to this office. |
| 54 | An Inventory & appraisement of the Estate of Jesse Lott, of 96 Districk, Intestate, made the 11th of January 1783 by James Fredrick, Hawell Johnston & John Fredrick, sworn appraisers. Sarah Lott, Admirx. Includes Negroes (not named). Total ₺ 1845 12 6.
N. B. No Return of Sale Made to this office. |
| 55 | An Inventory & appraisement of the Estate of Laughlin Leonard, late of the District of NinetySix, Intestate, made the 27th of December 1782 by Richard Griffin, Richd. Golding & Reuben Golding, Sworn appraisers. Mary Laughlin Admirx, of the Same. Includes Negroes Gorge[sic], Callo, Orange, Moses, Lett, Ben, Milly, Charles. Total appraisement ₺ 2649 3 0 in old currency. Examined & Certified by Pat: Calhoun, Surrogate
N. B. No acct of Sales of Said Estate returned to this office. |

Part of an Inventory & appraisement of the Estate of John Montgomery of Ninetysix District, Testator, deceased made by John McAlpin, Samuel Finley & William Martin appraisers, in & about the Month of February 1777 but the other part of the appraisement of said Estate

was Destroyed when said Samuel Finley's House was Burned by the Enemy, Certified the 6th of March 1783 by James Finley Exer, of the same. Total ₤ 102 10 0.
Examined & Certified by Pat: Calhoun, Surrogate

56-7 A List & Acct of the Sales of the Estate of John Montgomery, Deceased, made on or about the 25th of February 1777 and Certified & returned to this office the 12th of March 1783 by James Finley Executor, in old Currency. Purchasers: Andrew English, Wm Bob, Wm Strain, Henery Hay, Charles Hay, John Jonston, Hugh Reed, John McCalpin, Robart Selfrige, John Miller, John Pickens, Wm. Bell, Demsey Tyner, Thos. Bell, Joseph Pickins, Robt Young, Andrew Pickens, Shedrak Stevens, Thos. Hatcher, Aron Steel, Henry Peycock, George Alexander, John Strain, Thos Cannon, Joel Theaker, Joab Hatcher, Thos Coil, Joseph Pickins, Agness Mountgomery, Jas Filespey, Wm Lislly, George Willison, John McComb, Andrew Moat, Doctor Russell, Doctor Martin, James Seawright, Andrew Miller. Total ₤ 634 17 6. Examined & Certified by Pat: Calhoun, Surrogate.

57-8 An Inventory of the Estate of Robert Melvill, of Ninetysix District, Testator, deceased, as taken, Returned & Certified the 24th of June 1783, by Robert Maxwell, acting Executor of the last Will & Testament of the Robert Melvill, whos said last will Required neither appraisement nor Sale. Includes 200 acres on the waters of Turky [sic] Creek in Ninetysix District, 7 Negroes Viz Duncan, Charley, Jack, Bob, Joe, Bett & Sue. Cash on Hand viz Continental Paper Currency ₤ 11458 17 6 and South Carolina currency ₤ 1517.

58 A list or Schedule of Debts due to the Estate of the said Robert Melvill, Deceased. Accounts: Genl. Andw. Williamson, Lt. Col. John Purves, William Good, Doctor Timothy Russel, Wm Coffie, John Minter; Wm Lesley Juner a Note of Hand payable 23 March 1780; John McIlveney a Do. 6th April 1780; Joseph McLeskey a note payable 14 Oct 1779, one 20th Feby 1780, 9th July 1780; Danial Jones a Note of hand payable 23 Oct 1787; Mathew Gillespie a Do payable 16th Apl 1782; Wm Pickens note ditto payl. 2 July 1789; Mathew Cook, acct: Accounts due from Stephen Terry, Israil Pickins, William Gillespie, John Hearst, James Hammeger, Bartholomew Weems, Mr. Davies (Waggon Master), Henry Wyley, Mr. Zimmerman Senr, Samuel Gibson, Peter Knap, Lawrance Mark Senr, Patrick Do., John Anderson, Saml & Robt Anderson, John Allen, Henry Key. Total ₤ 8409 6 6.
Examined & Certified by Pat: Calhoun, Surrogate.

59 An Inventory & appraisement of the Estate of Jethro Roundtree, Intestate, made the 16th day of Decr 1782, by Benjn. Harris, Daniel Shaw, & John Sturzenegger, sworn appraisers. Jesse Roundtree, Admir. Includes Negroes America & Child, Sue, Isaac, Juda, Philis & Child, Barsheba, Lucy, Sam, Nance, Sam, Stephen, Agge. Total ₤ 3952 17 6. N. B. No Return of Sales of Sd. Estate to this office.
Examined & Certified by Pat: Calhoun, Surrogate.

59 An Inventory & Apprisement of the Estate of James Ray, Intestate, made the 20th of March 1783 by Joshua Hammond, James Christopher & Joseph Day, sworn appraisers. Abraham Richardson, Admir.
N. B. lands no right to be appraised
Land valued @ ₤ 77
Total amt. ₤ 92 7 6. N. B. No Sale of Said Estate returned to this office. Examined & Certified by Pat: Calhoun, Surrogate.

60 An Inventory & appraisement of the Estate of Christopher Smithers, Testator, deceased, made the 30th of December 1782 by Michael Mayer, John Tobler & Adam Hiles, sworn appraisers, John Sturzenegger, acting Exer. Includes Negroes Ned, Sanco, Dick, and 2 not named. Notes of hand of Samuel Sterk, David Zubly, Daniel Shaw. Total ₤ 3232 2 6.

N. B. No Sale of Said Estate returned to this office.

61   An Inventory & Appraisement of the Estate of John Scott, late of Ninetysix District, Testator, deceased, made the 5th day of December 1782 by James Thomas, Joseph Thomas and William Rennolds, sworn appraisers. Samuel Scott, acting Executor of the same. Includes Negroes: Lucy's child named Juda, Sely's child named Tom, Fanny's child named Becky, Fanny's child named Solomon, Hannah's child named Cate, Nell's child named Nancy. Total ₤ 2185 19 0. Examined & Certified by Pat: Calhoun Surrogate.

61-2 A list or Schudel of Accts & Debts due to the Estate of Sd. John Scott, deceased, taken the 3d of February 1783 by Samuel Scott, acting Exer and returned by him to this Office.
John Cook's bond dated 14th Decr 1779 due 1 Jan 1781
Andrew Moore's Bond dated the 28 Jan 1779, due 1 Jan 1781
Robart Bryans Note of ₤ 137 15 specee[sic] dated 17 Aug 1780.
Examined & Certified by Pat Calhoun, Surrogate.
N. B. No Sales of said Estate Returned to this office.

62   An Inventory & appraisement of the Estate of John Sanson of the District of Ninetysix, Intestate, made the 18th of January 1783 by Alexander Loggan, John Loggan, & David Logan, sworn appraisers. Jane Sanson, Admirx of the same. Total in old currency ₤ 265 17 6. Examined & Certified by Pat: Calhoun, Surrogate
(No Sale of Said Estate returned to this Office)

      An Inventory & Appraisement of the Estate of Isaac Tindsley, late of Ninetysix District, Intestate, made the 8th November 1782, by Richard Griffin, Anthony Golding & Reuben Golding, sworn appraisers, Elizabeth Tindsley, Admirx of the same. Includes Negroes (not named). Amount in old currency ₤ 1443 18 0. Examined & Certified by Pat: Calhoun, Surrogate. No Sale of Said Estate returned to this Office.

63   An Inventory & Appraisement of the Estate of Aaron Weaver, late of Ninetysix District, Intestate, made the 14th of Novr. 1782 by Russell Wilson, Lewis Clark & John Dugliss, sworn appraisers, Jane Weaver, admrix. Total ₤ 590 12 0.
Examined & Certified by Pat: Calhoun, Surrogate. No Sale returned to this office.

63-4 An Inventory & Appraisement of the Estate of John Wood, of Lawson fork, 96 District Intestate, made the 2d day of January 1783 by David Lewis, John Youn[g], & John Conner, sworn appraisers. Rebekah Wood, Admirx. Includes Negro woman, Poll.
A List of Accounts due the Estate of the within John Wood, also acct. of hard money. (No named given.) Examined & Certified by Pat: Calhoun, Surrogate.

64   An Inventory & appraisement of the Estate of James Wood, Esqr. of Lawsons fork, Nintysix District, Intestate, made the first of January 1783 by John Timmons, William Benson and William Thomson, sworn appraisers, Mary Wood, Administratrix of the Same. Includes Negroes Boub, Tomb, Dinah, Nancy, Mary, Betty, Lucy, Omey, Andrew, Adam, Cieley, Roase, Frank. Total ₤ 4472 5 0.
A List of Schudel of Open accounts due to Said Estate. (No names given) Examined & Certified by Pat: Calhoun, Surrogate.
No Sale of the above Estate returned to this office.

65-6 An Inventory & Appraisement of the Estate of John Williams late of Ninety Six District, Intestate, dated the 30th of April 1781. Total appraisement ₤ 507 9 0.

We do hereby Certify that the foregoing Inventory & appraise is a just
& true Copy as mentioned in the original, to the best of our knowledge
& belife, as there was not to our knowledge any Ordinary office held in
Ninetysix District at the time the original appraisement was made to
wit the 30th of April 1781, the Enemy being then in this District,
the Said Appraisement being then not made by Legale Authority, but of
Necessity, Certified by us (who then acted as appraisers) Given under
our Hands the 12th day of March 1783. Signed John Luckie & William
White.
Sworn to in the ordinary's office the 12th of March 1783, before me
Pat: Calhoun, Surrogate.
Examined & Certified by Pat: Calhoun, Surrogate.

66 A list of Schedule of Notes of hand & Accts belonging to the Estate
of the above John Williams, Intestate & is the amount of the Sales
at the Vandue of sd. deceased's Estate the first of March 1781.
Notes on John Verner, John McCurdy Junr., Wm Little (Miller), Alexander
Denham, John Kennedy, Henry McMurdie, Gorge Pettigrew, James Thomson,
Wm White, Israel Pickens, Wm Harris, Mary Price, Phillep Mathews,
Andrew Gillespie, Wm Elliot, Alexander Hall, Joseph McCluskey Senr,
Samuel Nelson, James Long, Samuel Foster, Wm Manson, Wm Baxter.
Amount in sterling Ł 93 19 11.
Certified & Returned into the Ordinary's Office the 12th of March
1783 by Israel Pickens Admir.
Examined & Certified by Pat: Calhoun, Surrogate.

67 An Inventory & Appraisement of the Estate of Josiah Allen, late of
Ninetysix District, Intestate, made the 13th of Septr. 1782, by
Russel Wilson, William Sisson & Enoch Grigsby, Sworn appraisers. James
Allen Admir.
[bottom half of page missing.]

68 An Inventory & appraisement of the Estate of Thomas Appleton, Intestate,
made the 17th of Septr. 1782 by David Zubly, Casper Nail & Daniel Shaw,
sworn appraisers. Joachim Bulow, Admir. Includes 6 Negroes (not named).
Total in sterling Ł 280 0 4. Examined & Certified by Pat: Calhoun, Surrogate. No Sale of Sd. Estate returned to this Office.

An Inventory & Appraisment of the Estate of James Adams Junr, late of
Cuffetown in Ninetysix District, Intestate, made the 28th day of September 1782 by James Harrison, Samuel Anderson & Benjamin Glanton,
sworn appraisers, Elisabeth Adams, Administratrix.
[remainder of page missing]

69 A list & acct of the Sales of the goods & Chattels of James Adams Junr
sold the 28th of Septr 1782 & Certified by James Harrison, Clark of
the Vandue. [Purchasers not listed.]

An Inventory & Appraisement of the Estate of James Adams, late of
Ninetysix District, Testator, made the 14th of May 178 , by Michael
Buckhalter, John Martin & Lewis Tilman, sworn appraisers. Drury Adams,
Exer of the Same. Includes Negroes Pahnney, Jiney, Roger, Jack, Jude,
Quash, Patt.
[remainder of page missing]

70 An Inventory & Appraisement of the Estate of Elisha Brooks Intestate,
made the 26th of June 1782 by Bartlitt Satterwhite, Morris Guinn &
John Caldwell, sworn appraisers. Frances Brooks, Admirx. Includes
Negroes Mager, Joe, Peter, Mingo, Sarah, Going, Bridget, Jinny,
Lewis, Hannah, James, Santy, Sylvea. Total Ł 5542 0 0.
Examined & Certified by Pat: Calhoun, Surrogate. No Return of Sale
made to this office.

[   ] appraisement of the Estate of Robert Boyd
[   ] -trict, Testator, Deceased made the 27th
[   ] aisers, William Hays Exer.
[balance of page missing]

71 Total appraisement Ł 152 11 0. Examined & Certified by Pat: Calhoun, Surrogate. No Sale Returned to this office.

71-2 An Inventory & appraisement of the Estate of Arthur Boyse, late of Ninety Six District, Intestate, made the 14th of June 1782 by John Wilson, George Reed, & James Seawright, Sworn appraisers, Alexander Boyse, admir. of the same. Total Ł 508 2 3. Examined & Certified by Pat: Calhoun, Surrogate. No Sale Returned.

72 An Inventory & appraisement of the Estate, of James Buttler, late of Ninetysix District, Intestate, made the 6th of Novr. 1782 by William Sisson, Joseph Nunn & Enoch Grigsby, sworn appraisers, Russell Wilson, Admir. of the same. Total Ł 103 7 8. Examined & Certified by Pat: Calhoun, Surrogate.

72 A list of the Sales of the Estate of James Buttler, sold the 22d of March 1783. Certified by Russell Wilson, Admir. [Purchasers not listed]. Total Ł 125 2 6.

73 An Inventory & Appraisement of the Estate of Robert Bryan, late of Coffee Town, in the Distirct of Ninetysix, Intestate, made the 30th of May 1782, by Samuel Anderson, James Harrison & Benjamin Glanton, sworn appraisers, Sarah Bryan, Admirx. of the same. Includes Negroes Jack, Prince, Shus (wench), Total Ł 2296 17 6. Examined & Certified by Pat: Calhoun, Surrogate.

A list of the Sales of the above Estate, sold the 30th of May 1782 and Certified by John Stewart, Vandue-Master. [Buyers not listed]. Total Ł 5475 0 0.

74 An Inventory & appraisement of the Estate of James Chiney, late of Ninetysix District, Intestate, made the 2 d of July 1782 by John Gray, James Thomas & John Turner, sworn appraisers. John Chiney, Admir. Pricilla Chiney, Admirx. of the same. Includes Negroes pompey, Isaac, Bettey, Peggy & hir child. Amount Ł 1149 5 -. No Sale returned. Certified by Pat: Calhoun, Surrogate for John E. Colhoun, Esqr., ordinary.

An Inventory & appraisement of the Estate of James Carter, late of Savannah River & District of Ninetysix, Testator, made the 31st of August 1782 by Samuel Wimbish, Peter Stubbs & Alexander Clark, sworn appraisers. Thos. Carter, acting Exer, of the same. Includes Negro Harry. Total in old currency Ł 499 2 6 + sterling Ł 71 6 0 3/4.

75 A Second Inventory & Appraisement of the goods & Chattels of James Carter, Deceased, made the 22d of December 1786 by John Cowan, William Clark & Alexander Clark, sworn appraisers. Thos. Carter, Exer. Lettice Mcfarlen formerly Carter, Exerx. Includes Negroes Theeney, Solomon, Nell, Tom, Jude, Lize, Lilley, Lucey, Edenborough. Amount in sterling Ł 616 7 0; N. B. The Sale of Said Estate not Returned to this office. Examined & Certifid by Pat: Calhoun, Surrogate. John Thomas Junr., Esqr. Ordinary. See page 12 of this book.

An Inventory & appraist. of the Estate of John Calhoun Sinr, Intestate, made the 25th of Octr. 1782 by John Wilson, Wm. Calhoun, John Irwin, & Victor Mathews, sworn appraisers. Catpn. John Calhoun Admir. Amount in old currency Ł 321 7 6. N. B. No Sale Returned to this office.

76	An Inventory & appraisement of the Estate of John Dick of Beech Island, in the District of Ninetysix, Testator, made the 10th day of Decr. 1782 by Michael Meyer, John Sturzenegger, & Nathl. Howell, sworn appraisers, Mary Dick Acting Executricx. Includes Negroes Sam, Augustine, Prince, Lunnen, Phebee, Sylvia, Sarah, Rose. Total ₺ 5946 4 0. No Sale Returned. Examined & Certified by Pat: Calhoun, Surrogate for John E. Colhoun, Esqr., Ordinary.
77-8	An Inventory & appraisement of the Estate of Benjamin Durborough, late of the District of Ninetysix, Intestate, made the 17th day of July by Thos. Wilson, William Robison, and Isaac Crowther, sworn appraisers, in three sheets of paper all of the Same date & signed by the said three appraisers. Mary Durborough, Admirx of the same. Includes a Negro Jack, 3 cows & 3 Calves betwixt James Mayson & B. Durborough. Total ₺ 1348 17 0. Examined & Certified by Pat: Calhoun, Surrogate for John E. Colhoun, Esqr., Ordinary. N. B. No Sale of Said Estate Returned to his office.
78	An Inventory & appraisement of the Estate of Burditt Eskridge, late of the District of Ninetysix, Testator, Deceased, made the 5th day of Septr 1782 by William Sisson, David Nicholson & John Daviss, sworn appraisers, Encoh Grigsby & Jacob Smith, Exers of the same. Includes Negros Will aged 25 or 26 years; Jane about 35 years; child Ruth daughter of Jane, 9 years old; child Barbe daughter of Jane, 6 years old, child Rose, daughter of Jane 3 years old. Total amount in old currency, ₺ 2110 5 0. Examined & Certified by Pat: Calhoun, Surrogate for John E. Colhoun, Ordinary.
79	An Inventory & appraisement of the Estate of Richard Evans, late of the District of Ninetysix, Intestate, made the 8th of Octr. 1782 by Henry Jones, David Bowers & Adam HIles, sworn appraisers. Tememia Evans, Admirx. Includes Negroes Peter, Patt, Sue, Will, Roben, Molley, Nanny, Mulattoes Daniel, Mall, Amy. Total in Sterling ₺ 1240 10 6. Debts due to the Estate include Martha Hall, for Negroes Bridget, Amy, Nancy.
	An Inventory & appraisement of the Estate of Edwin Ferned [ ] Horns Creek 96 District, Intestate made the first day [ ] October 1782 by William Jones, Joseph Millar, & Thomas [ ], sworn appraisers, John Rainsford, Admir. Total in South currency ₺ 69 5 0.
80-82	An Inventory & Appraisement of the Estate of George Galphin, Esqr., late of Silver-bluff, in the District of Ninetysix, Testator, with a list or Inventory of the Bonds and Notes of hand, etc. due to said Estate, made the 16th of May and 9th of September 1782 Certified under the hands and Seals of Stephen Smith, Robert Hankinson & Alexander Newman, Sworn appraisers, as was shewn to them by William Dunbar & Thomas Galphin, acting Executors of the same. Includes Negroes Jamey, Juney, Cyrus, Billy, Pumkin, Jess, Jacob, Foot, Old Cato, Cyrus & wife Maria & 5 children, James, Celia, Elsey, Amy, Judy, Charlot. Bonds etc. on Stephen Smith, Hugh Short, Lieut. Thos Vernor, Mich: & Abram Odam, Hezekiah Wade, Thomas Wattes, David Zubly, Joseph & Isaac Perry, Thomas Filpot, Titus Hollinger, William Davis, John Greenaway, Gasper Strouble, Jane Barnard, Henry Bell, George Foreman, Richard Brown, Alexdr. Lamar, Stephen Forrester, Philip Halveston, Estate of Edward Barnard, John Sellers, Titus Hollinger, James Habersham, Isaac Perry & Co., Isaac Odam, John Dupee, Thomas Rae, Henry Wimberly, John Wood, John Murray, Patrick Butler, Henry Bell, Catharine Shaw, Benjamin Bird, David Alexander, William Goodgion, Henry Mills, John Pigg, Hezekiah Wade, Joseph Bentley, William Oats, Abraham Spears, Elijah Wasdon, Peter Durowzeaux, William Barnard, John Rattam, George Newman, Patrick Butler, Joseph Marshall, Samuel Brunston. Francis Settles, George Walker, David Irvin, William Grif-

fin, John Jordon, William Tinley, John Tannes of Bryar-Creek.
Total ℔ 29389 14 7.

A List of Negroes that has absented themselves from the State & went
off but is Shortly Expected back when the Value shall be Assertained
and Sent to be offixed to their Names. Cloe & 5 children, Trump & his
wife Tennah, her daughters Hannah & Lenday, Sam, Vienace. Also a
Number other gon off with the Brittish & to the Indian Nation which
we dont Remember.

83   [first part of page missing]
     [Estate of Sharshall Grasty]
     Includes Negroes James, Phil, Charles, Tiney, Jane, Winny, Dick,
     Beck. Total ℔ 3954 4 6.

84   [first part of page missing]
     [Estate of William Golightly]
     Includes Negro Amos, Mulatto Dick, Negro Pricila, Lyda.
     Carried forward: ℔ 3130 2 0. [Total would be on the next page, the
     first part of which is missing]

85   [first part of page missing]
     Total ℔ 179 17 6. Examined & Certified by Pat: Calhoun, Surrogate for
     John E. Colhoun, Esqr., Ordinary.

86   [first part of page missing]
     [Estate of John Hearst]
     Total ℔ 803 9 0.
     A Memorandum of Debts to the Estate of John Hearst deceased. [No
     names listed]. August 19th 1779 paper Money 180 12 6. Total ℔ 1059
     7 6.

87   [first part of page missing]
     [Estate of William Hallum]
     Jenney Hallum acting Exerx of the same. Total ℔ 122 17 6.
     Examined & Certified by Pat: Calhoun, Surrogate, for John E.
     Colhoun, Ordinary.

88   [first part of page missing]
     [Estate of James Hall]
     and Isaac Hendricks, sworn appraiser, Mary Hall, Admirx. of the same.
     Includes Negro Man Morris. Debts due from John Blith of Georgia,
     Nicholas Holly.
     N. B. lands & ready money should not be appraised. P. C.

89   [first part of page missing]
     [estate of Edward Issom]
     Total ℔ 149 18 3. N. B. No Sale returned to this office of sd. Estate.

90   [first part of page missing]
     [estate of William Little, Jr.]
     [apparently a list of debts due:] William McElwee, Andrew Edwards,
     William McCarley, Charles Holland, Thomas Mann, William Turk, Thomas
     Edwards, James Chalmers, James Baker. Total ℔ 504 4 -.
     N. B. No Sale of Said Estate Returned to this office.

[Pages 91-94 are missing]

95   An Inventory & appraisement of the Estate of James Magill late of
     Ninetysix District, Testator, deceased, made the 24th day of October
     1782, by Richard Griffin, Anthony Griffin & Richd. Golding sworn
     appraisers. Anthony Golding Exer of the same. Total ℔ 93 0 0.
     N. B. No Sale returned to this office.

95-6	An Inventory & Appraisement of the Estate of James McKinly of NinetySix District, Testator, Deceased, made the 9th day of August 1777, by John Bell, James Caldwell & John Bole, sworn appraisers, by virtue of a power of appraisement to them directed by William Burrows, Esqr., then Ordinary in Charlestown, and dated 26th July 1777. William McKinley and Francis Carlile Exers of the Same, who made Return into this the 30th of Novr. 1782 to be record. Total ₺ 860 2 6. A list in Notes & Book Accts and Ready Money received by William McKinley & Francis Carlile, Exers. Pd. William Calhoun for writing the will. Bill of James Carlile. Paid to the orphants [sic] of James Carlile. to 42 days going & returning from Virginia for a Bond entred into by James Mckinley to Samuel Paxton concerning the Orphans from the 25th Novr 1777 to the 5th Jan 1778. [The will of James McKinley recorded in Charleston Will Book TT, p. 476.]
96	An Inventory & Appraisment of the Estate of William Norris late of the District of Ninetysix, Testator, deceased, made the 22d of Novr [ ] by James Fedrick, Howel Johnston & William [ ]. [remainder of page missing]
97	Total ₺ 2195 19 6 [probably belongs to the estate of William Norris] An Inventory & appraisement of the Estate of Samuel Patton, late of the District of Ninetysix, Intestate, made the 3d day of September 1782 by Peter Stubbs, William Hays and James Noble, sworn appraisers, Arthur Patton Admir. of the same. Includes Negroes Jack, Philles, Jane, Jack (again), May. [Total not given]
98	An Inventory & Appraisement of the Estate of JosephRice late of the District of Ninetysix, Intestate, made the 3d of October 1782 by John Gray, Conrad Gallman & Samuel Walker, sworn appraisers. Harmon Gallmon & William Brown, Admirs. Includes Negro Gabe. Total in old currency, ₺ 613 2 6. A list of the Sales of the goods & Chattels of the above Intestate Joseph Rice, the 13th of Octr. 1782. [purchasers not listed]. Total ₺ 668 0 0. Notes of hand to the above Estate. 1779 Septr 29th Owen Odom, May 3d Ephraim Rees, Decr 30th Thos Jones, Abraham Tylor & Elisha Tylor, Octr 1779 James Harris, Oct 3d 1779 Col. John Purves. The above is a Just & true Record taken from the original appraisement The list of Sales and list of Notes of hands due to the Estate of Joseph Rice Intestate as Returned to this Office. Examined & Certified by Pat: Calhoun Surrogate, For John E. Calhoun, Ordinary. [remainder of page missing]
99	Total appraisement [carried over from preceding page] ₺ 2536 10 6. Examined & certified by Pat: Calhoun, Surrogate.
99	An Inventory & appraisement of the Estate of Thomas Strain late of the District of Ninetysix, Intestate, made the 9th day of January [ ] by William Drennan [ ] and [remainder of page missing]
100	Total appraisement ₺ 392 11 6 [brought over from preceding page] An Inventory & appraisement of the Estate of John Taylor, late of the District of Ninetsix, Intestate, made the 25th day of July 1782, by William Hill, James Hogin & John Gorman, sworn appraisers. Heney Taylor, Admix of the same. Includes Negroes James, Dick, Nanne, Bob, Mitley, Stephen, Jane. Total in old currency. ₺ 2279 12 6. [remainder of page missing]

101   An Inventory & appraisement of the Estate of James Wilson, late of
      the District of Ninetysix, Intestate, made the 16th day of July 1782,
      by Alexander Boyse, George Reed, & James Seawright, sworn appraisers,
      John Wilson, Admir., Martha Wilson Admirx. of the same.
      [bottom of page missing]

102   An Inventory & appraisement of the Estate of Robert Wallace of
      Cuffetown Creek in Ninetysix District, Intestate, made the 22d of
      June 1782, by James Harrison, Benjamin Glanton, and Samuel Anderson,
      sworn a-praisers. Issable Wallace Admirx. of the same.
      Total ₤ 1185 5 0. Includes Negroes Friday, Fillice.

      A list of the Sale of the above Estate dated the 22d of June 1782.
      [Purchasers not listed]

      [bottom of page missing]

103   [end of estate begun on preceding page] Total ₤ 4547 15 0.

103-4 A list or Schedule of Book accts & notes of hand due to the Estate of
      Michael Watson, deceased, Certified the 21 day of Novr by Arthur Watson,
      Exer & Martha Watson, Exerx of the same. Notes on John Hall,
      Jacob [   ], John Rivers, James Kirkland, Jacob Adams, Wm Clark,
      John Salters, Samul Williams, Benjamin Lovless.
      [entire above entry stricken]

104-6 A list or Schedule of the Books Accts & Notes of hand due to the
      Estate of Michael Watson, deceased, certified the 21 day of Novr. 1782
      by Arthur Watson, Exer., & Martha Exerx of the same.
      Notes on John Hall, Jacob Watson, Daniel Hartle Senr., Samuel Tomkins
      (Dead), Benjn Tutt, Robert Melton, Field Perdue, Thomas Weems, James
      Buttler, Daniel Shoemat, Samuel Stalmaker, Charles Harrison, Robert
      Barlow, William Lareymor, James Ferrel, William Cammel, John Johnson,
      Elijah Bayley, Richard Johnston Senr., Ephraim Prescott (Dead), Ogdon
      Cockeroft, John Watson, James Buttler, Willis Watson, Jesse Lott (Dead),
      Robert Stark, Gabriel Fridig, James Roquemore, James Scott, Bentley
      Stocks, Job & John Red, John Sawyers, Henry Buzbee, John Robeson, James
      Marlen, John Cook, Thomas Wood, William Thompson, Jesse Parten, Charles
      Boyl, George Warren, Daniel Shaw, Richd. Levins, Coweatling Adams, John
      Sawgens, Buckner Pelman, John Jones, Gardner Williams, James Barronton,
      Lewis Watson, Martha Watson received of Sarah Lott, Elisha Brooks, John
      Higgains, John Hartly, Cash pd. James Moore, Edward Pines, Joseph
      White, John Sawyers, John Watson Junr. Cash pd. Samuel Stewart, Samuel
      Williams, Christopher Salters, James Harrison, Michael Ward, Howel
      Johnston, David Gains, Edward Couch, Frederick Hartly, James Warren,
      James Prichard, Henley Webb, Total ₤ 4440 6 11.
      Examined & Certified by Pat: Calhoun, Surrogate, for John E. Colhoun,
      Esqr., Ordinary.

106   An Inventory and appraisement of the Estate Charles Williams late of
      Stevens Creek & District of Ninetysix, Intestate, the 3d day of Sept
      1782, by Ebenezer Starns, Joshua Gray & Thomas Freeman, sworn appraisers.
      Celia Williams, Exerx[stricken] Admirx. of the same.
      [remainder of page missing]

107   [probably continuation of estate of Charles Williams]
      Total ₤ 1949 13 6.
      Examined & Certified by Pat: Calhoun, Surrogate for John E. Colhoun,
      Ordinary.

              [pagination recommences for Will Book]

NINETY SIX DISTRICT WILL BOOK

[Pages 1 through 12 are missing]
[Page 13 is blank]

14 SOUTH CAROLINA
In the name of God Amen. I George Galphin of the
Province aforesaid, Gentleman, do make this my last will and
Testament in manner and Form following, First it is my will that all
and every the Legatees herein after named or mentioned who are not
free shall from and immediately after my Death be and remain forever
free and discharged from all and all manner of Slavery and Bondage,
particularly I will that my muletto Girl Named Barbara be free and I
do hereby give her her freedom, Also I give to my muletto Girls
Rachel and Betsey (Daughters of a muletto woman named Sapho) their
Freedom, Also I give to my half breed Indian Girl Rose (Daughter of
Nitehuckey) her freedom and also five Cows and Calves and two mares
and Colts, and my will is that they severally shall be forever free
and discharged from all Bondage and Slavery. Also I give and devise
to Thomas Galphin Son of Rachel Dupee all my household Furniture and
plate and Ten mares and Colts and all the riding horses belonging
his and his Sisters Cowpen in Ogechee with the half of all Stock of
Cattle at Ogechee aforesaid with his and his Sisters Mark and Brand,
likewise all Cattle and Horses with his own Mark and Brand. Also I
Give and devise to the said Thomas Son of the said Rachel Dupee (without
Impeachment of Wast) for and during the Term of his natural life
the use Occupation and Enjoyment of my Grist Mill and Saw Mill, Situate
lying and being on the North side of Town Creek together with all
the lands on the Same Side of Said Creek Containing about one thousand
acres, also the use of my new Brick House with four hundred acres of
Land belonging to it and all the Imporvements thereon Situate in the
province of South Carolina Also the use of all the land from Mr. Shaw's
lower line upon Savannah River at the Spanish Cutoff down said River to
Mr. McGillvery's lower line containing about one thousand three hundred
acres in the province of Georgia Also one tract of land on the out
side of the Swamp in said province of Georgia which I bought from James
McHenry, Also two thousand acres of Land of the Ceded Land in any part
he may Chuse that belongs to me or may belong to me Also three hundred
and fifty acres of Land upon Ogechee which I bought off Patrick Denneson
Also a tract of land on the Back Swamp in the said province of South
Carolina, containing four hundred acres, all without Impeachment of
of waste, Also the use work and Labour of the following Slaves (that
is to say) Petersisom and his wife Nanncy their Children and future
Issue, Cato his wife Bess their children and future Issue, Syefa
Negro man, Joe and Cornelia his wife their Children and future Issue
Kelly, Tom his wife Lucey their Children and future Issue, Michal his
wife Sarah their Children and future Issue, Coffe his wife Betty their
Children and future Issue, Goodfellow (a Negroe man), Sarah I had off
James Deveaux, her Children and future Issue, Little Frank (a mustee
Boy), Davey (A Negroe Man), Pompey and his wife Sarah and Issue, Rachel
(Fridays wife), her children and future issue, and upon the Death of
the Said Thomas I give my said Mills, Brick House and all the said
15 Lands and Slaves with their future Issue unto the Child or Children of
the Said Thomas that shall be then living in such parts and proportions,
and for such Estate and Estates, and at and under Such Limitations, Restrictions
and Contingenies as he the said Thomas Shall by his last
will & Testament in writing or by any deed by him to be duly Executed
in his lifetime direct limit or appoint, and for want of Such direction
limitation and appointment I give and bequeath the said Mills, Houses,
Lands and Slaves and their Issue to and amongst all and every of the
children of said Thomas that shall live to come of age or have Issue
to be Equaly divided amongst them and their respective Heirs and assigns

forever as Tenants in Common and not as joint Tenants, and if but one
Child of the Said Thomas Shall live to come of age or have Issue then to
that Child alone and to his or her Heirs and assigns forever; Also I give
and bequeath to Martha Galphin (Daughter of the Said Rachel Dupee) for and
during the Term of her Natural Life without Impeachment of waste the use
of two Tracts of Land Containing five hundred acres each, Situate lying and
being above Mr. Raes above Augusta in the Province of Georgia Also the use
of two Lots of Land in Augusta Also fifty acres of Land in Augusta which
I bought of John Joachim Zubly where Gray lived with all the Improvements
thereon, Also one tract of Land on the outside of the Swamp I bought off
Wade joining McHenry's Land in the Said Province of Georgia, Also two
thousand acres of the Ceded Land in any part She may that belongs or may
belong to me all without Impeachment of waste Also I give & devise unto
the said Martha Ten Horses and Seven mares with the half of all the Stock
of Cattle at Ogechee aforesaid her and her Brothers Mark and Brand likewise all Cattle and Horses with her own Mark and Brand. Also the use work
and Labour of the following Slaves (that is to Say) Dick his wife Clerarda
their Children and future Issue, Billey his wife Dina their Children and
future Issue Dutch-Jemmy, Beckey her children and future Issue, Jemima her
Children and future Issue Deborah and her future Issue, Gwind Tom his wife
Juba their Children and future Issue, Trump his wife Tina their Children
and future Issue, French Peter his wife Silvia their Children and future
Issue, and little Jacob and upon the Death of the said Martha, I give all
the said Several tracts and lots of land last above mentioned unto the
Child or Children of the said Martha (together with the last mentioned
Slaves and their Issue) that shall upon such Contingency be living in Such
way and manner parts and proportions and for such Estate and Estates and
at and under such Contingencies Limitations and Restrictions as the said
Martha shall by her last will and Testament in writing or other writing by
her duly executed directed limited and appoint, and for want of such direction limitations or appointment I give and bequeath the said Several
Tracts and Lots of land last above mentioned and the said last named
slaves and their Issue and Increase to and among all and every the Children of the said Martha [that shall live to come of age or have]

16   Issue to be equally divided amongst and their respective Heirs and Assigns
forever as Tenants in Common and not as joint Tenants, and if but one
Child of the said Martha shall live to come of age or have Issue then to
that Child alone and his or her Heirs and Assigns forever. Also I give
to George the son of Metawney (an Indian woman) Ten Horses and Seven mares
with the one third of all the stock of Cattle, with his own and Sisters
Judith's and Brother John's Mark and Branch wheresoever they be found,
likewise all Cattle and Horses with his own Mark and Brand, Also I give
and bequeath unto the said George for and during the term of his Natural
life without Impeachment of waste the old Brick House with one hundred
acres of land whereon it stands, also two hundred acres joining, one hundred acres more joining all below said Brick House in said province of
South Carolina, Also all that tract of Land containing five hundred acres
above the Spanish Cutoff on Savannah River in the province of Georgia
Also I give and bequeath unto the said George and John his Brother the
Saw Mill on the South side of Town Creek with the Tract of land whereon it
stands containing about one hundred acres together with all the land I Run
upon the South Said[sic] of and joining the said Creek above the Said Saw
Mill containing about one thousand acres to hold to them jointly, Also I
give to the said George two thousand acres of the Ceded Land in any part
he may chuse[sic], that belongs or may belong to me, to be disposed of as
he the said George shall think proper, Also I give the said George the
use work and Labour of the following slaves (that is to Say) Coboy, his
wife Sarah their Children and future Issue, August a Muletto man and his
Children except Rose whos freedom I have herein given, Moll her Children
and futur Issue, Ingston, his wife Darkey their Children and futur Issue,
Gray's March his wife Claranda and any Issue she may have by him, Sue her
Children and future issue, Joe his wife Hannah their Children and future

Issue, Long John his wife Sarah, their Children and futur Issue, Leander, Frank and Harry and upon the Death of the Said George, I give the said Brick House with the said one hundred acres of Land whereon it Stands, and the sd. two hundred acres joining one hundred acres more joining, all below the said Brick House with the said Tract of five hundred acres; Likewise his Joint part of the said Saw Mill with the said one hundred acres of Land; with the Joint part also of the said one thousand acres of land, And also the Slaves and their future Issue unto the Child or Children of the Said George that then shall be living in Such parts and proportions, and for Such Estate and Estates and at and under Such Limitations Restrictions and Contingencies as the said George shall by his last will and Testament in writing or by any Deed by him to be duly executed in his life time direct limit or appoint and for want of directions limitation and appointment I give and bequeath [the Said Brick House and Land, with his Joint part of] the
17 said Saw Mill and Joint part of the Said Lands there after mentioned and the Slaves and their Issue to and amongst all and every of the Children of the said George that Shall live to come of age or have Issue to be equally divided amongst them and their respective Heirs and Assigns for ever as Tenants in Common and not as Joint Tenants and if but one Child of the Said George shall live to Come of age or have Issue then to that Child alone and to his or her Heirs and Assigns for ever. Also I give to John (Son of the Said Metawney) Ten Horses and Seven Mares with the one third of all the Stock of Cattle with his own sister Judith's and Brother George's Mark and Brand wheresoever they may be found, likewise all Cattle and Horses with his own Brand and Mark Also I give and bequeath unto the said John for and during the Term of his natural Life without Impeachment of waste the Tract (or Tracts) of Land upon Ogechee in the province of George called the old Town which I Run out Containing about One thousand one five hundred acres, Also that tract of land below it that was John Sallers's Also that Tract of land in the Swamp called Dunifin's Place which I bought off him Also two Hundred acres of land which I run out joining it with the tract of land I bought off Joel Walker behind it; Dunifin's place fronting the River Also I give and bequeath unto the said John and the said George his Brother the Saw Mill on the [South side of Town Creek with the tract of land whereon it Stands Containing about one hundred acres together with all the land I run up the South side of and joining the said Creek above the said Saw Mill, Containing about one thousand Acres, to hold to them jointly] Also I give to the said John two thousand acres of the Ceded land in any part he may Chuse that belongs or may belong to me, to be disposed of as he the said John shall think proper, Also I give to the said John the use work and Labour of the following Slaves (that is to Say) Stepney his wife Margret their Children and future Issue, Phina her Children and future Issue, Mingo his Wife Maria her Children and future Issue, Ockera his Wife Cate their Children and future Issue Limerick, King, Nero, Negro Men, Colo peter a Negro man, Olipher his wife Cresha their Children and futur Issue, New Negro Dick, Peter (I bought of Joseph Butler) his wife their Children and future Issue, Sapho (a Muletto woman) her Children and future Issue (except her Daughters Rachel and Betsey whom I have herein before made free), New Negro Jack, Bulley, and Chevers, Negro Men, also Delia a half Breed Indian woman, she to serve him seven years, then to be free, and the said John on the day of her freedom to give her five Cows and Calves, And upon the Death of the said John I give the said several tracts of land, together with his joint part of the said Saw Mill and tracts of land thereafter mentioned, and also the Slaves and their future Issue Unto the Child or Children of the Said John that shall be then living in Such parts and proportions and for Estate and Estates and at and under such Limitations Restrictions and Contingencies as he the Said John shall by his last Will and Testament in writing or by any Deed by him to be duly executed in his life time direct limit and appoint, and for want of Such [remainder of line missing]

43

18   -pointment I give and bequeath the said Several tracts of Land together
with his joint part of the said Saw Mill and Tracts herein before Mentioned, with the Slaves and their futur Issue to and amongst all and
every of the Children of the Said John that shall live to come of age or
have issue to be equally divided amongst them and their respective Heirs
and assigns for ever as tenants in Common and not as Joint tenants, and
if but one Child of the said John shall live to come of age or have Issue
then to that Child alone and to his or her Heirs and assigns for ever.
Also I give unto Judith (Daughter of the Said Metawney) for and during
her natural life (without Impeachment of waste) the use of the upper half
three tracts of land, which said tracts run from Mr. Newman's line down
to the point, Containing in the whole about **thirteen** or fourteen hundred
acres with the Dwelling House and all other Improvements thereon where
she now lives Called Silver Bluff in the province of South Carolina
Also I give to the Said Judith Two thousand acres of the Ceded land in
any part she may Chuse that belongs or may belong to me, to be disposed
of as she shall think proper, Also I give and devise unto the said Judith Ten Horses and Seven Mares, with the third of all the Stock of
Cattle wheresoever they may be found, with her own, her Brother George's
and her Brother John's Mark and Brand, likewise all Cattle [and Horses
with her own Mark and Brand, Also the use work and labour of the following Slaves (that is to Say) Warick his wife Marcha their Children and
future Issue, Billey, Peter and Cela (Mustees) her Children and future
Issue, Sally an] Indian wench her Children and future Issue Kelly's
Abraham his wife Elcey their Children and futur Issue Cyrus his wife Sue
their Children and future Issue, Joe his wife Emma their Children and
futur Issue, Old Cyrus his wife Maria their Children and future Issue,
Gabriel his wife Minerva their Children and future Issue, Jacob his wife
Cloe their Children and future Issue, Charlotte her children and future
Issue, and upon the Death of said Judith I give the use of the said Upper
half of the said three tracts of land with the Dwelling House and Improvements and Slaves with their future Issue; Unto the Child or Children of
the said Judith that shall be then living in such parts and proportions
and for such Estates and Estates and at and under such Contingencies
Limitations and Restrictions as the said Judith shall by her last will
and Testament in writing or other writing by her duly executed direct
limit and appoint, and for want of such direction limitation and appointment I give and bequeath the said uper half of the said three tracts of
Land with the Dwelling House and Improvements and the sd. Slaves last
mentioned with their future Issue to and among all and every of the
Children of the said Judith that shall live to come of age or have
Issue to be equally divided amongst them and their respective Heirs
and assigns for ever, as Tenants in Common and not as Joint tenants, and
if but one Child of the said Judith shall live to come of age or have
Issue then to that Child alone and to his or her Heirs and assigns
[part of line missing] Barbara (the Daughter of

19   [part of line missing] [during her Natural life] [part of line missing]
[waste] the use of the lower half of] three Tracts of land which said
Tracts run from Mr. Newman's line down to the point Containing in the
whole about thirteen or fourteen hundred acres with all the Improvements
thereon called the Silver Bluff in the Province of South Carolina, Also
I give unto the said Barbara Two thousand acres of the Ceded land, in
any part she may Chuse that belongs or may belong to me to be disposed
of as she shall think proper. Also I give and devise unto the said Barbara Ten Horse and Seven Mares Likewise all Cattle and Hoses with her
own Brand and Mark, Also the use work and Labour of the following Slaves
(that is to Say) Little March Katte (that was his wife) their Children
and futur Issue Ponpon Jemmey, his wife Betty their Children and future
Issue, Ned and his Sister Dido (son and Daughter to Dido deceased)
her Children and future Issue, Bidgo, Sib his wife, Young Sib her Children and future Issue Indian Peter, his wife Capuchey their Children and
future Issue, and Georgia Dublin, And upon the Death of the said Barbara

44

I give the use of the said lower half of the said three Tracts with the
Improvements and Slaves with their future Issue unto the Child or Children of the said Barbara that shall be then living in Such parts and proportions and for such Estate and Estates and at and under such Contingencies Limitations and Restrictions as the said Barbara shall by her
last will and Testament in writing or other writing by her duly executed
directed limit and appoint and for want of such direction limitation and
appointment I give and bequeath the said lower half of the said three
Tracts of land with the Improvements and the said last mentioned Slaves
and their future Issue to and amongst all and every of the Children of
the said Barbara that shall live to Come of age or have Issue to be
equally divided amongst them and their respective Heirs and assigns for
ever as Tenants in Common and not as Joint Tenants, and if but one child
of the said Barbara shall live to come of age or have Issue, then to
that Child alone and to his or her Heirs and assigns forever, Also I
give to the said Thomas a Negro   man named Abraham which I had
off Mr. Barnard, also Indian Prince, under the same Restrictions with the
rest of the slaves hereinbefore mentioned. Also I give unto the said
Thomas all my great Guns, with my Silver mounted Gun and pistols, the
rest of my Guns I give to the said George and John equally between them,
Also it is my will that in Case any of the Six Devisees and Legatees
herein before mentioned, namely George, Thomas, John Judith, Martha,
Barbara, shall happen to die without leaving Issue or their Issue die,
that then and whenever a Contingency of that kind happens to any of the
said Devisees or any of their Issue that the Estate, Slaves and Issue of
Slaves hereby intended for such Devisee or Devisees and Issues shall be
shared equally by my Executors or the Survivors of them amongst the Survivors of the Said Six Devisees and Legatees, and the Lands to be Shared
between [the said George] [remainder of line missing][and their Issue to
be [remainder of line missing]]Devisees and Legatees and their Heirs
Likewise it is my will that the Six Devisees and Legatees shall during
their respective minorities be respectively maintained Clothed Schooled
and educated out of the profits of the Estate hereby intended for them
respectively, and that upon any of their Deaths leaving Issue living,
such Issue shall during their respective minorities be maintained Cloathed
Schooled and educated out of the Issues and profits to arise out of the
Estate, and Labour and Services of the slaves hereby intended for such
Issue, Also I give unto the said Six Devisees and Legatees all my Sheep
to be Equally divided between them and after my Debts and the other Legacies to other persons herein after mentioned shall be paid and delivered, I give and devise all the rest residue and remainder of my real
and personal Estate of what nature or kind soever and wheresoever to
and between the said Thomas and Martha and their Chidlren Share and Share
alike and in case the Said Six Devisees and Legatees should all Die Intestate and without Issue I leave all the Estate hereby given to them
among my Sisters and their Heirs Share and Share alike. Also I give to
David Holms five hundred pounds sterling also two Tracts of Land on the
long Reaches where Galfin lived and one Tract on the long Reaches in the
Georgia side I Bought off Benjamin Stedham and two thousand acres of the
Ceded Lands, to him and his Heirs in Lieu of any part of my Estate he may
lay Claim to, I leave to Judith Galphin my Sister one hundred and fifty
pounds Sterling, in Lieu of any part of my Estate She may lay any Claim
to, I leave Catherine Galphin living in Ireland One hundred and fifty
pounds Sterling, in Lieu of any part of my Estate She may lay any Claim
to, I leave to My Sister Margret Holms Fifty pounds Sterling, to each of
her Children now in Ireland Fifty pounds Sterling and to her son Robert
now living here fifty pounds Sterling and one thousand acres of the Ceded
Lands, in Lieu of any part of my Estate they or any of them may lay Claim
to, I leave to Mrs. Taylor Fifty pounds Sterling, also five hundred
acres of the Ceded Lands to each of her Children also five Cows and Calves
to each of them in Lieu of any part of my Estate she or they may lay
claim to, I leave my Sister Crossly fifty pound Sterling, a paceing horse
and a new Side Saddle in Lieu of any part of my Estate She may lay any

Claim to and each of her Children Fifty pounds Sterling and five hundred Acres of the Ceded Lands, with a Horse and Mare to each of them in Lieu of any part of my Estate they may lay Claim to, I leave to my Cousin George Rankin in Ireland Seventy pounds Sterling to him or his Children in lieu of any part of my he [sic] may lay Claim to, I leave to George Newman Fifty pounds Sterling and a Horse of the value of Ten pounds Sterling in Lieu of any part of my Estate he may lay Claim to, I leave to my Aunt Sennard's Daughter in Ireland to her and her Children fifty pounds Sterling in Lieu of any part of my

21 [Estate She or they may lay Claim to, I leave to my] Cousin John Foster, fifty pound sterling to him and his Children in Lieu of any part of my Estate he or they may lay Claim to, I leave to Rachel (Daughter of Sapho) herein before mentioned Two negro men and two Negro Women to be bought out of the first Ship that Comes in with negroes, Ten Cows and Calves, three Mares and Colts One Horse and twenty pounds Sterling, also that tract of land where John Raton lived Called Clouds place between Macbean and Briar Creek to her and her Children but if She Dies without Children then to her Sister Betsey (Daughter to the Said Sapho) I leave to the Said Betsey one new negro man and woman to be bought her, Ten Cows and Calves two mares and Colts, one Horse, and that tract of Land below the Cowpen on Macbean to her and her Children but if she dies without Children then the whole to fall to the said Thomas(son of the said Rachel Dupee) and his Children to be maintained and Schooled on the plantation until they are Married or of age and then to receive what is left them. I leave to Betsey Callwell (Daughter of Mary Callwell) one New Negro winch, Ten Cows and Calves, Two Mares and Colts one Riding Horse and Saddle and that tract of land at the three runs at the old Stomp above Tims Branch and Fifty pounds Carolina Currency to be laid out in Cloathing, for her the whole to be put in her own possession after my Death to her and her Children. I leave to all the poor widows and fatherless Children within Thirty miles of where I live in the province of South Carolina [and Georgia, Fifty] pounds sterling, I leave Fifty pounds Sterling to be Shared among the poor of Eneskilling and Fifty pounds Sterling to be Shared among the poor of Armagh in Ireland; I leave to Timothy Barnard Two hundred pounds Sterling, I leave to all the Orphan Children I brough up Ten pounds Sterling each and Billey Brown to be bound out to a Trade; I leave John McQueen and Alexander his Brother each a good riding Horse and each of them and their wives a Ring, I leave to Mr. Netherclift and his wife each a Ring, I leave all my Executors a Suit of Mourning and a Ring each, I leave to Mr. and Mrs. Wylly each a Ring, I leave to their Daughter Suckey Wylly Fifty pounds Sterling and a Suit of Mourning, I leave to each of my Sisters their Husbands and Children a Ring, I leave to Mrs. Campbell a Ring, I leave to Mr. Cartan Campbell a Ring, I leave to Mrs. Frasier a Ring and Ten pounds sterling, I give to Mr. Newman a Ring and twenty pounds Sterling, I give to the widow Atkins twenty pounds sterling and a Ring. I give to her two sons William and Alexander each a good riding Horse, and to her Daughter I give a good pacing Horse of the Value of ten or twelve pound Sterling. I give to Mr. and Mrs. Greirson each a Ring, I give to person Seymor and his wife each a Ring, I give to George Parsons a likely Negro Boy to be bought him out of the first ship that Comes in, and one of my best riding Horses. I leave to Quinton Pooler five hundred acres of the Ceded Lands, and to all the rest of my Cousin Poolers (man and Woman) each

22 a Ring [in Lieu of any part of my estate they may lay Claim to I leave to the Said] Rachel Dupee the use of one Negro man Called Foot, one Negro wench called Charlott and her Children during her Natural life and then to her Son Thomas, and that her Son Thomas and her Daughter Martha are to pay her twenty pounds Sterling Yearly as long as She is Virtuous or lives single, and then to leave her ten Cows and Calves and Martha's Negro Boy called Jacob as long as they think proper, and they may let her live upon any of their land, I leave her also a paceing Horse and side Saddle, also one Bed, one pair of Sheets, three Blankets, two Counterpins, one set of China Cups and Saucers, Tea pot and Tea Kettle, the

rest of the Cups Saucers Kettles and soforth together with the plate that is in the House, and all my other plats and so forth I leave to the said Thomas and Martha, Also I leave to each of the said Six Legatees a Bed and furniture, I leave my Sister Young in Ireland, Fifty pounds Sterling, to each of her Children fifty pounds Sterling and to each of them five hundred acres of the Ceded Lands and five Cows and Calves and a Horse and Mare to each of them in Lieu of any part of my Estate they may lay Claim to. I give to Clotworthy Robson five hundred acres of the Ceded Lands to him and his Heirs, I give to each of the Six Legatees first mentioned a Stallin to Run with their Mares (three of the likeliest to the Boys and three Jack Asses) and as Soon as they or any of the Said Six Legatees shall arrive at the age of twenty one years or be Married which ever shall first happen I will that he She or they shall Immediatly have [possession of all the Estate hereby given to him her or them]. I give to all my Hunters and House wenches a Suit of Mourning to all the Cowpen wenches, and a New Shirt and shift to each of the rest of my Men and Women Slaves; I will that the said Metawney do live at her said Children's Cowpen and be maintained and Cloathed by them, and I give to her and the said Rachel Dupee each a Suit of Mourning, and that the said Thomas, Martha, and John be sent to Charlestown or Savannah to School; And in case there is not sufficient to pay of the said Legacees I will that all the reaminder of my Horses, Mares not herein willed and Lands be sold, and the profits of the Saw Mills and work of all my slaves be applayed for that purpose, after the maintainance Schooling and Cloathing of the said Six Legatees. Also I will that the said Thomas and Martha may dispose of their tracts of the Ceded Lands as they shall think proper. And Lastly I do hereby nominate Consistute and appoint James Parsons, John Graham, Lauchlin McGillvery Esqrs., John Parkinson Mect., the said George, Thomas and John Galphin's and the Survivors and Survivor of them Executors and Executor of this my last Will and Testament and Guardians of the Real and personal Estates hereby given to the said Legatees and in Case the said George, Thomas and John or any of them shall be under age or incapable of acting at the time of My Death, that then they shall (with the Consent of the other Executors) Nominate and appoint other Persons to act in their stead until such Time as they Come of age or are Capable of Acting. In Witness Whereof

23 I have to this my last Will and Testament Contained in nine sides of papers set my hand and Seal the sixth day of April in the year of our Lord one thousand Seven hundred and Seventy Six
Signed sealed published and
decleared by the said Testator George
Galpin as and for his last Will and Testa-   George Galphin
ment in the presence of us who in his   Seal
presence and at his Request have sub-
scribed our Names as Witnesses hereto
        David Zubly
        Michael Meyer
        John Sturzenggar

I the within Named Goerge Galphin do make and publish this Codicil to my Last Will and Testament in manner following (that is to Say) I do hereby revoke that part of my will wherein I bequeathed to the within named Judith and Barbara the three Tracts of Land between, I bequeath to the said Judith the place whereon she now lives adjoining John Newman's land, containing three hundred acres under the Contingencies Limitations and Restrictions mentioned in my last Will, I revoke that part of my will wherein I bequeath to the said Judith the Negroes old Cyrus, his wife Maria her Children and futur Issue I revoke that part of my will wherein I bequeath to the within named Martha the Negroes Ned, his wife Jamima her children and future Issue, French Jemmey his wife Cassandra her Children and future Issue, I bequeath the said old Cyrus his wife Martha her Chilren, the said Ned (Called Cut Nose) his wife Jamima her Children and future Issue to my Sister Martha (the wife of William

Crossley) during her natural life and after her decease to be equally
divided among her Children Share and Share alike in Lieu of any part
of my Estate she or they may lay Claim to, I revoke that part of my
Said will wherein I leave David Holms the land on the Long Reaches that
Golfin lived on, two tracts in Carolina and one in Georgia on the long
Reaches (which I bought off Benjamin Stedham) I leave the said Tracts of
Land to my Sister Martha Crossley during her Natural life and after her
decease to be equally divided among her Children Share and Share alike
in Lieu also of any part of my Estate she or they may lay Claim to,
I revoke that part of my said Will wherein I leave several parcels of
the Ceded Lands as Legacies to different persons In Lieu thereof I leave
to each of the said Legatees the Sum of Fifty pounds Sterling, I leave
to my Sister Young in Ireland and to each of her Children the Sum of
Fifty pounds Sterling over and above what I have left them in my foregoing
Will, I leave the Negro Simon to the within named Thomas Son of the within
Named Rachel Dupee, And in Case I shall Sell any of the said Lands or
Slaves herein before bequeathed my Will is that the Monies arising from
Such Sale Shall be paid to Such person or persons to whom I have herein
or in my said Will bequeathed Such Land, Slave or Slaves so Sold, I re-
voke that part of my said Will wherein

24 I leave to the said Barbara that Land below Silver Bluff being a part of
three Tracts of Land and in Lieu thereof [   ] her that whole Tract adjoining the point containing upwards of three hundred acres, the lowermost
part of said Land, the Land between the two parcels I left to the said
Judith and Barbara I leave to the said Thomas Son of the said Rachel Dupee,
I revoke that part of my said Will wherein I leave a Negro named Tom to
the said Barbara as he belongs to the within named John son of Metawney
by virtue of a Bill of Sale to him from Lauchlin McGilvery Esqr and
whereas in and by My Said Will I have given and bequeathed the Sum of
fifty pounds Sterling and a Horse to George Nolin, I do hereby order
and declear that my will is that only the sum of Five Shillings Sterling
be paid to him in Lieu of any part of my Estate he may lay Claim to,
I do forgive David Holms aforesaid all the Money he may be indebted to me
at my decease in Lieu also of any part of my Estate he may lay Claim to,
Also I forgive Timothy Barnard all the Money he may be indebted to me
at my decease, Also I leave to George Grierson the youngest son of Mr.
James Grierson the Sum of One hundred pounds Sterling And it is my will
that none of the Legatees in my said Will or herein mentioned be paid to
any of the legatees until such Legatees shall first give a Discharge
in full against any Claim every such Legatee may have to any part of my
Estate And Lastly I nominate constitute and appoint William Dunbar of
Silver Bluff an Executor of my said last will [and of this Codicil in
Conjunction] with the other Executors in said Will nominated and it is
my desire that this my present Codicil be made a part of my Said last
will and Testament to all intents and purposes, In Witness whereof I
have hereunto set my hand and Seal this fourteenth Day of February in
the year of our Lord one thousand Seven hundred and Seventy eight.
Signed Sealed published and Decleared by the within Named
George Galphin a Codicil to his last Will and Testament
in the presence of
    Jonah Horry   George Galphin   Seal
    David Zubly
    Clotworthy Robson

I the said George Galphin do Make and Publish this Codicil also to my
last Will and Testament in manner following (that is to Say) I give
Brin (the Son of Hannah a Negro wench) and Sally the Daughter of
Clarissa (a Muletto wench) their Freedom together with Ten Cows and
Calves to each of them and also Two hundred acres of land to each of
them of Some of my lands not herein already divided, whereas I have
forgiven David Holms, and Timothy Barnard all the Money the may be
indebted to me at my deceased I desire it may not extend to any Debts
they may be owing in England, whereof I am Security, but only such

25 private Debts as they may be owing to myself, Revocke that part of my will wherein I bequeathed the Negro little March to the said Barbara, I give and bequeath the said Negro little March to my Sister Crossley. In my said will I have given and divided Unto the said Thomas and Martha (after my Debts and Legacies are Paid) all the rest and residue of my Real and personal Estate, I now give and devise all such residue and remainder of my Real and personal Estate unto the said Thomas Martha and John (the son of the said Metawney) and to their Children Share and Share alike. I give and bequeath unto George Mary and Fenry Crossley the Sons and Daughter of my said Sister Crossley one hundred and fifty acres of Land (which I bought of one Friar) on Savannah River in Georgia and two hundred acres in South Carolina on said River opposite the said one hundred and fifty acres and to their Heirs forever and in Case I should sell the same I then leave to each of them the said George Mary and Fenry Crossley the sum of One Hundred pounds Sterling in Lieu of any part of my Estate they may lay Claim to And it is my desire that this present Codicil be made a part of my Said last Will and Testament to all intents and purposes, In Witness whereof I have hereunto set my hand Seal this Sixteenth Day of March, in the year of Our Lord one thousand Seven hundred and Eighty

Signed Sealed and Delivered by the Said
George Galphin as a Codicil to his last   George Galphin (Seal)
Will and Testament, in the present of
   Wm. Harding
   Richd. Henderson
   Clotworthy Robson

I the said George Galphin do make and Publish this Codicil also to my last will and Testament in manner following (that is to Say) I revoke that part of my will wherein I left to Betsey (the Daughter of the Said Sapho) who is Since dead one New Negro Man and Woman to be bought for her, Ten Cows and Calves, Two Mares and Colts, One Horse and that tract of land below the Cowpen on McBean, I leve the Same to William Holms, in trust for his son Thomas and to his the Said Thomas's Heirs and assigns forever. I also revoke that part of my last will wherein I left to the Said George the Negro Moll her Children and future Issue, I give and devise unto the Said Barbara (the Daughter of the said Rose deceased) the said Negro Moll her Daughter Judey and her Child Sam her Son, Lucy and the rest of her Children and the future Issue of the Moll and her Daughters unto the said Barbara her Heirs and Assigns for Ever. In Lieu whereof I leave and bequeath unto the said George, Young Sibb her Daughter and future Issue, Ming, Elsey, their Children and future Issue (and Ketch a Boy) for Ever. I revocke that part of my said will wherein I left George Nowland only five Shillings and desire he may have what is mentioned in the said Will. In Witness whereof I have hereunto Set my hand and Seal the Twenty Sixth Day of September in the year of our Lord one thousand Seven hundred and Eighty
Signed Sealed published and decleared by the Said George Galphin as a Codicil to his last will and Testament in the presence of
Before Signing the Said George Galphin
26 desires that none of the Negroes may have any Mourning or anything else (on account of their Ingratitude)except Kelly's Dick and Tina

   John Anderson   George Galphin (Seal)
   Michael Walsh
   Clotworthy Robson

The foregoing writting from page 14 of this Book is a just & true Record taken from the Original Will and Several Codicils, of the above Named George Galphin deceased, which said Original Will & Codicills was duly probated, in the Ordinary's Office, the 6th day of April 1782. On the Oaths of John Sturzenegger and Clotworthy Robson two of the Subscribing Witnesses to the said Will & Codicils, taken before John Ewing Colhoun,

Esqr., Ordinary of the District of Ninety Six. Examined & Certified by Pat: Calhoun, Surrogate.

27 Will of John Dick of [Gran]ville County in South Carolina, 20 April 1776, all my Estate shall remain in the hands and Possession of My well beloved Mary my wife...she shall live for the support of her and her Small Children. I leave with her and after her Death it is my will that my Land whereon I Dwell and a Negro fellow Named Sam Shall be my son Joseph's, My other Lands to be Occupaid[sic] for the support of my young Children untill they are grown up and married, and then to be divided, My three Sons, William, John and Thomas, my other Negroes to labour in the aforesaid land for the support of the aforesaid [   ] hands of my Son Joseph after the Death of his Mother, if it shall Please God to spear him and he Shall Support his Sisters untill they are grown up to provid for themselves, as for my stock of each kind being but small it is my will they be divided between my four youngest Children, My Negroes all but Sam after the girls are married...my wife with Joseph my son to be my Lawful Executors...21 April 1776
Witnesses Ann Newman
           John Newman   John Dick (Seal)
           Alexander Newman

The Original Will of John Dick was duly probated by Alexdr. Newman one of the above Subscribing Witnesses before John Ewing Calhoun, Esqr., Ordinary of 96 District the 8th day of April [   ].

28 Will of Robert Boyd of Gra[nville] County in the Province of South Carolina....to my well beloved wife Mary Boyd, 200 acres of land with the improvement I have made, during the time of her widohood, next I give and bequeath to my son Robert Boyd two hundred acres of land with the improvements over by the old Spring, Next I give and bequeath to my Daughter Agnes Boyd one hundred acres of land with the improvements formerly belonging to Hugh Calhoun, and next I give to my wife Mary Boyd one Bay Mare and with a snip in his face; And next I give to my son Robert Boyd one Mare and Colt branded with V S, and Next I give to my Daughter Agnes one Mare Colt with a star in its face, and next I give to my Son William Boyd three Dollars, and all the rest of my Goods and effects to be divided equally between my wife Mary Boyd and my son Robert Boyd and my Daughter Agnes Boyd, after all my just Debts and funeral Charges are paid...friends William Hays and Patrick McMaster Executors... 21 June 1779
Wit: Robert Boyd   Robert Boyd (RB) (Seal),
     Patrick McMaster

The above is a true Records taken from the original Will and Examined by Pat: Calhoun, Surrogate.
The Original Will of the above Robert Boyd deceased was duly probated by Robert Boyd one of the Subscribing Witnesses before John Ewing Calhoun Esqr., ordinary of Said Ninetysix District the 20th April 1782.

28-9 South Carolina, Ninetysix District. Will of James Adams...to wife Sarah use of all my Estate; to sons namely Thomas & Drury one tract of land Containing one hundred acres lying on both sides of Horns Creek said land was first granted to Hall Summeral, said land to be equally divided unto them and their heirs for ever. I Give and bequeath unto my son Littlebury all that part of my land that lyes between Rambo's land and the first branch on East side of said branch Runing from the mouth and bounding to the head of Said branch, and then a Strate Course to the back line, to him & his Heirs for ever. I also give my son Littlebury one Negro boy named Roger to him and his Heirs for ever, and if my son Littlebury should die without lawful Heirs, his land and Negro Roger I give unto my son Benjamin & I give and bequeath unto my son Benjamin all that part of my lands Inclosing the plantation lying on the West side of

a branch that leads to Rambo's---also Negro boy Isaac to him and his
Heirs for ever and if my son Benjamin should Die without Lawful Heir,
his land and negro and Negro boy Issaac I give them unto my son Littlebury, and if my son Littlebury and my son Benjamin Both should Die
without Heirs lawfull Begotten of their Body, their lands and Negroes
namely Roger & Issaac I give to be Equally divided unto all my Children
I give and bequeath unto my Daughter Sarah one Negro Boy named Quash.
I give and bequeath unto my Daughter Elisabeth one Negro Girl named
Patt, to my daughter Rachel, one Negro Girl name Jude, unto my Children
and Grand-Children namely James deceased his Child, my son John's
Children, my Daughter Mary's Child, my son Thomas's Children, my Son
Drury's Children & Rebeck's my Daughter's Children, Two Negroes Namely
faney & Jane and their future InCress together with all the Negroes
I shall get or purchase hereafter. and after my wife Sarah is deceased
I give and bequeath unto my Children namely Littlebury, Benjamin,
Sarah, Elisabeth and Rachel all my stock of Cattle, Horses, Sheep,
Hoges & Household furniture to be Equally divided to them...sons Thomas
and Drury Executors and wife Sarah Executrix, 14 October 1781.
Wit: John Herndon   James Adams (J) (Seal)
    John Goldin
    Benjamin Mossley (P)
    Hannah Mossly ( )
The Original Will of James Adams was duly probated by Benjn Mossly on
    [remainder of page missing]

30   Will of James Norrell of the District of Ninetysix and State of South
Carolina, 12 August 1779....
to my well beloved wife Mary Norrell all my Real and Personal Estate
During the time she Remains my widow and after she Marrys to be Divided as Follows---to my son Isaac Norrell one Sorrel Mare Colt got by
Mark Antony; to my son Levy Norrell my present Dwelling Plantation
whereon I now live containing 126 acres...all the Residue and Remainder
of my Estate consisting of three Negroes, Horses, Hoges, Cattle,
Household furniture, etc. be sold and equally divided Share and Share
alike between my wife aforesaid and my sons Isaac Norrell, Jacob Norrell, and James Norrell and Levy Norrell, and my daughters Martha Norrell, Elizabeth Norrell and Mary Norrel...wife Mary Extx and [   ]
haniel Spraggins, Esqr., and my son Isaac Norrell Exrs...
Wit: Richd. Allison   James Norrell (X) (Seal)
    Wm. Anderson
    Samuel Abney
The Original Will of the above James Norrell was dully Probated by
Richard Allison one of the subscribing witnesses to said Will, before
John Ewing Calhoun, Esqr., Ordinary of Ninetysix District, the 26th
day of April 1782. The foregoing writing is a true Record taken from
said Original Will Examined by Pat: Calhoun, Surrogate.

30-1   [pages in poor condition]
Will of William Golightly of Fairforest in South Carolina and Nineth
[sic] District, 18 Jan 1782...to wife Amey Golightly, possession of all
my Real and Personal Estate during widowhood, and afterwards I leave
my Negro man [   ] to my son Cristopher Golightly and negro Abraham
to son William Golightly, to son David negro Dick; To my two daughters
Clairmon and Mary [   ]; to my Loving Brother David Golightly, three
hundred pounds, wife Amey and Brother David Exrs.
Wit: Charles James   William Golightly
    Moses Foster
    John Foster
The original Will of the above named William Golightly was duly Probated by Mosser[sic] Foster one of the Subscribing witnesses to said Will,
before me in the ordinary's office the 31st July 1782. The foregoing
writing is a true Record taken from said original will, Examined by
Pat: Calhoun, Surrogate.   A copy given to the Exor.

32   South Carolina, Ninetysix District, Will of Michael Watson of the
      District Aforesaid...to wife Martha Watson, part of the tract [   ]
      live on to contain 300 acres, except my land on Clouds [Creek?] be Sold
      and the Money divided between my four [   ]...to my son Eliga Watson,
      that tract of land on Clouds Creek joining land of Warren Cusach & Allen
      containing [   ] hundred and fifty acres...to my wife during her
      [   ], for the Support of my Children all my Personal Estate, but
      [   ] of them Marry or Come of age during that time then my will
      is the Executors should make an equal division...wife and friends
      [   ] Watson and Robert Stark, Exrs., 26 May 1782
      Wit: Robert Stark
           Wm. R. Withers   Michl. Watson (Seal)
           Richman Watson
      The Original Will of the above Michael Watson was duly Probated by
      Richman Watson one of the Subscribing witnesses to the said Will be-
      fore me in the ordinary's office of Ninetysix District the 22d of
      July 1782.
      The foregoing writing is a true Record taken from the original Will,
      Examined by Pat: Calhoun Surrogate. A Copy Given to Exerx.

33   Will of Burditt Eskridge of Colliton[sic] County, Ninetysix District in
      the Province of South Carolina, being well in health....23 March 1779....
      to my loving wife Nance the third of all the Land I Possess During her
      Life; to my eldest son Samuel that Land as lyes on Red Bank; to my
      second Son Grigesby so Called the land that was Surveyed for James
      Smith joining Enoch Grigesby; at my wifes Decease her thirds of the
      Land I leave to my son Richard; I desire that my Negroes shall be e-
      qually divided at my son Samuel's coming of age, the Child that my
      wife is now with is to have an equal part of the Negroes and at my
      wifes Death an equal part of her thirds of the Negroes, if the Child
      that my wife is now with is a Boy each of my sons must pay him one
      hundred pounds a Piece Currency, my wife Enoch Grigsby & Jacob Smith,
      Exrs....
      Wit: Jno David
           Jacob Smith   Burditt Eskridge (Seal)
           Sarah Smith
      The original will of the above Named Burditt Eskridge was duly Probated
      by John Davis one of the subscribing Witnesses to said Will, before me
      in the ordinary's office the 20th day of August 1782.
      The foregoing writing is a true Record taken from said original Will,
      Examined Pat: Calhoun, Surrogate.

34-5 Will of Laurence Rambo in the District of Ninetysix in Granville County
      and province of South Carolina, planter....to my eldest son Reuben Rambo
      five Shillings Sterling of Great Britian; to my second son Laurence
      Rambo a certain Tract of Land being part of three Tracts of Land two
      two of the tracts surveyed by myself and one of the said Tracts
      surveyed by Joseph Nobles, containing or supposed to Contain one
      hundred acres with the Mill Dwelling House and all the Buildings there-
      on, beginning at a Corner Tree surveyed by Walter Jackson upon my
      Springs Branch, Mill Creek, Nobles line, Rogers corner, also a tract
      on Dry Creek part of 750 acres surveyed for myself adj. John Cockbourns
      line, where it cuts the Reedy branch, William Mosely's line; to my
      third son Benaja that part of a tract of land purchased of Joseph
      Nobles on the North side of Nobles Creek, that part of a 750 acre
      tract on the West side of Reedy branch not before devised to my son
      Laurens; to my fourth son Joseph Rambo the plantation whereon I now
      live with all lands not devised to my former sons; to my daughter
      Elender a Negro woman Hannah; to my daughter Elizabeth a Negro woman
      Judith; to my daughter Rebecca a Negro girl Tinner; to my daughter
      Margaretta a Negro Girl named Sabira; to my daughter Ruth Herendon
      the Negro child with which me negro woman is now pregnant; to my
      Loosing Daughter a Negro boy named Squash; to my wife Mary all my

Estate Real and personal; if my wife dies without marring then the Moovables not before bequeathed to be equally divided among my Sons and Daughters, and my Son Reuben's Children to have a Childs part to be equally divided among them; John Herendon and my son Laurence Rambo joint Exers..11 June 1775
Wit: John Rainsford   Laurence Rambo (Seal)
    John Roebuck (J)
    Rebekah Adames
The original will of the above Laurens Rambo was duly Probated by John Rainsford one of the Subscribing witnesses to the said Will, before me in the ordinary's office the 16th day of August 1782.
The foregoing Writing is a true Record taken from the said Original Will, Examined by Pat: Calhoun, Surrogate. 96 District Ordinary's Office.

36   Will of James Carter of South Carolina; to my loving wife the third of my estate during her life, then to be equally divided between my Children as they come to lawful age...my wife and brothers Thomas Carter and Robert Carter, Exrs, 9 Nov 1779.
Test: Benjamin Johnson (X)
      Thos Carter   Jams Carter (Seal)
      Sarah Carter.

The Original Will of the above James Carter was duly probated on the Oaths of Thomas Carter & Sarah Carter two of the Subscribing Witnesses to the said Will, before Robert Alexander and James Johnston, Esqrs., in Lincoln County in North Carolina, the second day of August 1782 by Virtue of a dedimus to them directed dated the 17th of June 1782. Certified in the Ordinary's office of Ninetysix District by Pat: Calhoun, Surrogate.
The foregoing writing is a true Record taken from the said Original Will Examined by Pat: Calhoun, Surrogate

36-7 Will of John Hearst of Ninetysix District and Settlement of Long Cane, 9th September 1780; unto my loving wife Mary Hearst, one third part of all my moveable Effects, and the full benefit of this House and Plantation where I now reside during her widowhood; to my son Robert Hearst and Daughter Mary Hearst, one Shilling Sterling if demanded; to my son John Hearst the sum of one Shilling Sterling, if demanded; and likewise to my sons Joseph Hearst, Thomas Hearst, George Hearst and William Hearst, to each of them one hundred acres of the Wood Land belonging to this Plantation as they come of age; if of my four youngest sons should Die Minors then his or their parts shall go to the Survivors of the four above mentioned; to my five daughters Christian Hearst, Elizabeth Hearst, Mary Hearst & Margaret Hearst & Ann Hearst, the remaining two thirds of my moveable effects; unto my three youngest Daughters one hundred acres of land I purchased from Jane Humphreys, to be sold and Equally divided amongst them over and above their parts of my Moveable effects this I give in Consideration of their youth and helpless Condition...to my step Daughter Elener O'Bryan, ₤ 23 Currency to be paid her when of age; wife Mary, sole Extx...
Wit: Chas Teulon   John Hearst (Seal)
    Robt Wilson (X)
    Robt Erwin (X)
The Original Will of the above John Hearst was duly probated on Oath of Robert Erwin one of the Subscribing witnesses to the said Will before me in the office of Ordinary the 23d of August 1782. The foregoing writing is a true Record taken from the sd. Original. Will Examined by Pat: Calhoun, Surrogate.

38 South Carolina, 96 District; Will of James Magill of the province and District aforesaid, being of Sound Memory, 8th Febry 1779...unto my Grand-Son James Golding one tract of Land 280 acres on a small branch of little River adjoining lands laid out unto Christopher Neelly and William Lowrey with two Negroes named Will & Wenn with all their future Incress, etc; unto my grandson William Golding the plantation where I now live on Containing 150 acres also two Negroes Moriah and Silvey with all their future Incress; to my Grand son Anthoney Golding one tract of land containing 220 acres laying on a Small branch of Saludy River called Cane Creek with two Negroes named Jack & Joe. I also give to my three Grand-sons above named one tract of land 207 acres laying on a Creek called Hoges Creek in Fredreck County, Viringia, to be sold and equally divided between my three Grand-sons, with all stock, etc; to my son in law Anthoney Golding all that lands I have in South Carolina the Benefit of untill my three Grand-sons comes of age; to my grand-son JamesGolding one Negro girl named Dinna; to grandson William Golding negro girl Hannah; to my nephew William Lowrey, all my wearing apparel; should my three grand-sons die & leave no heirs, the three parts of my estate should be sold and equally divided between my nephews in Ireland and America; friends Anthoney Golding, Robt. Cunningham, Willm. Oneal and Henry Oneal, Exrs....
 Wit: John Johnson
   George Potts   James Magill (Seal)
   Catherine Johnson (∅)

The foregoing writing is true Record taken from the original Will of the above James Magill, deceased' which said Original will was probated on the oath of John Johnson one of the subscribing witnesses to the said Will before me in the office of Ordinary for Ninetysix District the 24th of August 1782. Examined by Pat: Calhoun, Surrogate.

39-40 The State of South Carolina, Ninetysix Distrct; Will of James Moore.... to my beloved wife Anne Moore, my Negro man named Jack and Aaron, silvy and patience together with the use of my plantation and Horses, Household furniture and Stock of Cattle & Hogs during her life, and at her death to be equally divided among my children which shall be hereafter named also the work horses; to my first son Davis Moore, negro Boy named Bob, and Black Mare, also as much money to be Raised out of my estate by cropping or other wise as my Executors, to buy land for a plantation,for him to live on; to my second son James Moore, my Negro Boy named Joe and my Mare called the Black filley, and four or five hundred acres Good land to be bought to make him a plantation to live on; to my third son Jonathan Moore, negro Boy Charles, big white mare, with half the tract of land I now live on, to be divided by my executors; to my fourth son Wm. Drayton Moore, negro boy Allin, colt called Dred, and the other half of the Land I now live on; should my wife be with Child and brought forth living, I lieave it my Negro Boy Edmond, and a colt (if a son), and money to buy a tract equal with Davis or James above mentioned; I leave the Rest my Negroes with their Increse and the Rest of my Estate together now in Care of Mother Patt and those lent to my wife, between my Children, when ever Davis, comes to the age of 21 or should marry younger...I desire the Land joining of me formerly the property of Fredrick Glover, now Chiffill & Anerom to be Bought if possable and equally divided between Jonathan and Wm. Dreyton Moore together with the Land I now live on; I leave the use of my Negro girl Patt to my Mother Susanna Moore; wife Anne Moore with William Moore, John Moore and Richard Moore, executors; 12 Jan 1780.
 Wit: William Neal   James Moore (Seal)
   William Wilson (W)

The foregoing Writing is a true Copy or Record taken from the Original Will of the above named James Moore deceased, which was duly probated before me in the office of Ordinary for 96 District on the Oath of William Neal one of the subscribing witnesses the 23 of September 1782.

40-1 Will of Christopher Smithers of the Province of South Carolina, New-
Windsor Township, Carpenter, being very sick and weak in Body....
to Catharine my Dearly beloved wife, all my Household Furneture with
one half part of my Stock of Horses, Cattle, etc., also the use of my
Plantation and three Negroes named Ned, Jin, Phibe, and after her death
to be the property of my son James and his Heirs, on the provise that
James to the age of twenty one, or has Lawful issue of his Body; to son
James the remainder of my Negroes, Saneo, Dick and Cate, and the one
half of stock, etc....wife Extx during her widowhood only, and John
Sturzenegger and Lud Williams Exrs., 17 February 1781
   Wit: John Nail   Christopher Smither (X) (Seal)
         John Tobler
         William Shinholser
The foregoing writing is a true Record taken from the original Will of
the above named Christopher Smithers, deceased which said original Will
was duly probated on the oath of William Shinholser, one of the subscribing witnesses the 2d day of September 1782.

41-2 Will of William Golding of South Carolina, Ninety-six District....
to my son John Golding, the land & Plantation I now live on Containing
150 acres, also one tract of land lying & joyning between above said
land & Plantation & Col. James Williams mill containing 146 acres,
also one feather-Bed & furniture, also Five Negroes Doll, Lucey, Jack,
Harry, Hannah, with their increase; to my son Reuben Golding one tract
& plantation that I purchased of James Daniel, containing 300 acres on
little River adjoining the land I now live one, and negroes Joe, Joe,
and Cate with their increase; to my son Anthony Golding, one tract containing 200 acres which I purchased of Capt. John Caldwell on the N E
side of the land I now live one, also one Negro Jacob; to my son
Richard Golding one Negro named Lankister; to my daughter Mary Leonard
four Negroes, Callamy, Ben, Milley and Lett with their Increase; to my
son William Golding, two Negroes Wagoner and Lucy & their increase, he
has the said Negroes now in his possession; to my daughter Milley Griffin, one negro Jane and her increase, which she has in her possession;
to my daughter Sarah Foster, one Negro woman named Nan with her increase, she has in her possession; to my daughter Elisabeth Tinsley, one
Negro Woman named Jane & her increase which she has in her possession;
to my son Robert Golding, one Negro woman Nan, Boy Doss, and their
increase; remainder of stock, etc to my sons John and Reuben Golding;
John & Reuben named Exers.... 4 September 1777.
   Wit: James Griffin
        Laughlin Leonard   William Golding (W) (Seal)
        Peggey Golding (P)
The foregoing writing is a true Record taken from the Original Will of
the above William Golding which said original will was duly probated
on the oath of Peggey Golding one of the Subscribing witnesses on 23
Sept 1782. Examined by Pat: Calhoun, Surrogate.

43   Will of William Norris of the Province of South Carolina, Ninetysix
District, planter...to Agness my well beloved wife one third part of
my lands, Negroes, and all I possess as her absolute property, and all
the rest of my estate to be equally divided amongst all my Children,
but to remain in possession of my wife until my first Child becomes
of age, then to be divided and paid to my children as they marry or
become of age...wife Agness, Extx, and John Fedrick Exor....10 Feb 1781.
   Wit: Howell Johnston (Le)
        Joseph Abel (S)   Wm Norris (Seal)
        Elisabeth Norris (O)
The foregoing writing is a true Record taken from the original....
probated on the oath of Howell Johnston, 18 Oct 1782.

44-5 Will of William Hallum of South Carolina, Ninetysix District, planter, very sick and weak in Body....to my dearly beloved wife Jenney, the third of all my Clear lands during life and the House I now live in together with all my plantation Tools, etc.; also to her one negro Woman Cate, child Dinah, mare, cow, one gown pateren six or seven yards linen Cloath,all the yearn now in her possession; to son William Hallum, 100 acres of land to be taken of the west side of this plantation I now live on, one Negro Boy Peter, bed, gun, etc.; to my son James, 100 acres of land to be taken of the one side or end of the place I now live on; to my son Josiah 50 acres of land the remainder of said Plantation, also one milch cow; to my sons Thomas Hallum, Robert Pickens and his wife Dakos, two Negro girls named Mimy and Saly to be divided between themselves as they can agree best upon; to my daughter Martha, one Cow, one Womans Saddle tree with leather, etc; To Joseph Smith and Elisabeth his wife, I leave the sum of five shillings sterling; I give to my wifes son William Griffith one three years old Horse and one Saddle; to my wifes daughter Margaret Griffith, one Bed the property of my Wife before Marriage together; to my sons John, Thomas & William all my wearing apparel to be divided amongst them as equelly as they can themselves agree upon...wife Jenney Extx & son John Exor...9 January 1782..-.
Wit: Samuel Rosamond
    Josiah Downan   William Hallum (Seal)
    John Preter
The foregoing writing is a true Record taken from the original will... probated on the oath of Samuel Rosamond, 6 September 1782.

45-7 Will of James Crawford of Long Cane Settlement, Ninetysix District, and Province of South Carolina, free holder, though advanced in days, and weak in Body....to Elizabeth my Dear and loving Wife, the Dwelling House & Plantation whereon I now live with all my house hold furneture, during her Widowhood; to my youngest & well beloved son Thomas Crawford, all the plantation whereon I now live, at his mother's death or marriage, also two Negroes Sampson and Ebenezer, and his choice of my horses, watch and silver stock & shoe Buckles, also to further his education ₤ 1000 lawful current money of the Province; to my son William Crawford one Negro boy Nero, also my best suit of apparel; to my well beloved daughter Margaret Campbell, one mullatto winch Kate; to my beloved son John Crawford, one negro boy named Jack; to my daughter Martha Long one Negro child Phillis; to my son James Crawford one negro winch Hannah; to my daughter Elizabeth Turnbull, one negro woman named Phillis and her Child which she now has. My plantation on Rocky River containing 400 acres be sold at public vandue, and all stock except what is willed, and ₤ 1000 to be given to my son Thomas Crawford, and the remainder divided equally amongst all my Grand-children Male & Female every one an Equal share; Jesse Campbel, my son in law and Joseph Turnbull, my son in law, Exrs....7 November 1780
Wit: John Sprott
    Jno Cochran   James Crawford (Seal)
    William Alexander
By Misfortunes since my last Regulateing my worldly affairs it now Behoves me to make some Alteration in Respect of my Negroes, which hath been Violently taken from me...if they be regained they shall be Destributed as I have heretofore directed...25 December 1780...
Wit: Wm. Crawford
    Jesse Campble   James Crawford (Seal)
    James Crawford Junr.
The foregoing writing is a true Record taken from the original Will and Codicil of the above James Crawford, deceased, which the first part of said original will was duly Probated on the oath of William Alexander, one of the subscribing witnesses 4th February 1783 (the Codicil not probated as the subscribing witnesses thereto, are either gon as Enemies with the British or deceased). Examined by Pat: Calhoun, Surrogate.

Will of Richard Hughs, being in a low state of health....
my son Richard to have 100 acres of the old Place joining my Brother
William's Land, and 100 of the Bounty land adjoining the same; to my
wife Mary, all the Household stuff and Stock, to be at her Disposale for
the bringing up of the Child, and the Negroes at her deceased to be
Equally divided amongst my Children, the 200 acres Bought of Squire
Brown I give to my son John; the 100 acres of the old Place including
the Mill Seat I give to my son Joseph; the old Plantation adjoining
I give to my son William; Joshua Palmer and James Bogan, Exrs, 5 Apr
1781
Wit: John Allberten
     Jeptha Hollingsworth   Richard Hughs (LS)
     James Johnston
     James Bogan
The foregoing writing is a true Record taken from the above deceased
Richd Hugs Original Will, probated on the oath of James Bogan, one of
the subscribing witnesses 13th Febry 1783 before Pat: Calhoun, Surrogate.

48 Will of Thomas Pickett in the State of South Carolina, being sick and
weak in body...I give unto my Beloved wife Mille Pickett all my Estate
Moveables & Imoveables, during her Natural life and after her Decease
to be equally divided amongst my children by an euqal division...
William Runolds, and wife Mille Pickett, Exrs., 26 May 1782
Wit: Thos Rennolds   Thomas Pickett (LS)
     William Goode
Probated on the oath of William Goode the 24th February 1784 before
Pat: Calhoun, Surrogate.

48-9 Will of Robert Melvil of the District of Ninetysix, planter, and in
the State of South Carolina...I desire that my wife Mary may have a
Negro fellow named Duncan and a Negro woman named Bett, with what
Children they may have after the date of this writing, and my household goods, except one good Bed with furneture, with the use of my
Plantation as long as she lives unmarried, and at her marriage or
death to go to John Mcfatrick, with my stock of Hogs, I mean my Plantation to go to Mcfatrick; I desire that Robert Maxwell may have all
my Bodyly apparel, both made and unmade, both at white hall, at my
own Plantation & at Genls Williamsons Plantations, all my Books, and
indeed all I have in the world more than what I have mentioned above
except a Horse Saddle and Briddle, a Cow & Calf to John Miller, but
Miller to serve out his time first with Maxwell, and Negroes to
Maxwell Charles, Jack, Bob, Joe & Sue, and all debts due me...Mary
my wife Extx, Robt Maxwell & John Maxwell Exrs, 12th Septr 1782
Wit: Will Maxwell
     Nicolas Maxwell   Robt Melvill (Seal)
Original will probated on the oath of Nicolas Maxwell, 24th March
1783 before Pat: Calhoun.

49-50 Will of Andrew Burney, being very sick & weak in body....to my Step
son George Bender 100 acres of land adjoining Land formerly belonging
to his father and purchised by me from Joseph Wilson, also the following Negroes if he will receive the same in Lieu of what may be due him
from me, as likewise one half of all my Horses, Cattle, Hogs and Plantation tools (Negroes not named)...to Andrew, Thomas and William
Bassett Smith, the following Negroes (not named), as also one tract
of Land containing 550 acres adjoining lands of James Wilsons's on
Savannah River in the long reaches, as also one tract of land on Steph-
ens Creek, containing 200 acres, granted to Ulric Tobler & purchased
by me from his son J. N. Tobler, and one half of Horses, etc....
to my well beloved Sister Elisabeth Milling, two Lotts in the town of
Augusta known by No. 12 & 16 situate on Broad and Reynolds Streets,
and Negroes (not named)...freinds Mr. B. D. & L. W. to be Exers....
A list of division of negroes belonging to the estate of the said

Andrew Burney has annexed to the said Will is as followeth to wit
First division of Negroes No. 1 Cloe & child, Cyrus Jude Molley &
child, Judith & Cesar, Mode & Bob, boys [in margin: in Georgia]
Second division of Negroes, No. 2, for George Bender, Phebe, York,
Lucy, Sarah & Child, Mengo, ₺ 50
Third division of Negroes No. 3 for George Bender, Eve, Brister Jimm,
Brass, Jak & Eve, old Negroes ₺ 50
Negroes No. 4
Goodgs, Simon, Rockaman, Simon, Mode, Abram, Jemmie, Joe, Pender,
Sew & her three Children--Peter, Ned & Jenary, Jude, Violet; and
Member

The foregoing writting is a Just & true records taken from the Original
Will of Andrew Burney, probated on the oaths of David Zubly Sinr, and
Britton Dawson, who on their oaths decleared they were Called by the
Testator as Witnesses to the same, sworn to the 9th day of May 1782,
before John Ewing Colhoun, Esqr., Ordinary of Ninetysix District.

50   Will of William Gorden of Ninetysix District...
to my son William Gordon, 150 acres of land, part of a 200 acre tract
known as Fords Survey, not taking the Plantation; to my son John Gordon,
150 acres of land joining George Gordon's line, part of the tract where
I now live, Runing up & down the River; to my son Posey Gordon, 150
acres of land joining the other part of the same tract I live on; to
my daughter Cassey Gordon the Plantation where I now live, the remainder of my land with 50 acres joining part of Fords Survey; to my loving
wife Elizabeth Gordon, all my Negroes to wit, Bob, Sam and Venus,
during her widowhood and after to be equally divided among my four
children, William, John, Posey, and Cassey...wife Elizabeth Gordon,
and Thomas Gordon and Gabrel Anderson, Extx & Exors, 19 Apr 1781...
Wit: William Cureton
      Thomas Perey (Y)   William Gordon (Seal)
      Penelepe Perey (X)
Probated on the oath of Penelepe Perey, the 7th day of November 1782,
before John Ewing Colhoun, Esqr., Ordinary of the District of Ninetysix.

51-2 Will of John Hogg of the State of South Carolina, and the District of
Ninetysix, farmer, 14th July 1781....
to my well beloved son Lewis Hogg, one tract of land lying on the Sd.
side of Enoree River, containing 150 acres, formerly the property of
John Clark; to my two sons Thomas Hogg & Stephen Hogg, the plantation
or tract of land that I now live on to be equally divided between them
when they Come of age, containing 200 acres; to my son John Hogg, 100
acres of land lying on the Sd. side of Enoree River formerly the property of Captain Charles King; to my son Joseph Hogg, one Eighty Gallon
still, also one tract of land that I bought of Joseph Readin if it can
be procured; to my son Zachariah Hogg, and grand-son Frances Hogg, the
tract of land my son James Hogg, formerly lived on Containing 150 acres
to be equally divided between them; I will that my wife Sarah Hogg,
shall live on the plantation that I now live on During her life or
pleasur and my furniture and Stock to be kept together for the support
of my family and Children, & each Child to have an equal part as they
come to age; son Lewis Hogg and Sarah Hogg, my wife, Exors...
Wit: Thomas Wafer
     William Darby (W)   John Hogg (J) (Seal)
     William Sparks
Probated on the 8th day of November 1782 by the oath of William Sparks,
taken in the Ordinary's Office before John Ewing Colhoun, Esqr., Ordinary of the District of Ninetysix.

52-3 State of South Carolina, Will of John Scott of Granville County in the
State aforesaid, being of Sound mind tho weak in Body....

58

to Samuel Scott my eldest son, 300 acres of Land, in Richmond County
in Georgia, granted in my Name 4th of May 1773 bounded by vacant land
at the time of the Survey, also the nineteen following Negroes Solomon,
Fanny, Judy, Patty, Pompey, Sely, Molly, Seipio, Saff, Peter, Nancy,
Hannah, Big Dick, Lucy, Dinah, Billy, Friday, Gadow, Phillis, likewise
one half of all my moveable effects, Horses, cattle, Sheep, etc., and
one half of the cash I may die possessed off; to James Scott, my Youngest Son 200 acres of Land on Savannah River in Georgia, granted to me
in two tracts of 100 acres each and joining each other, both Grants
dated 5th July 1774, and 19 negroes Major, Sary, Kate, Jenny, Joe,
Betty (a Child), Harry, Curry, Edy, Little Dick, Andrew, Nell, Jeffry,
Lucky, Tony, Jack, Betty (a Woman), Henry, Frank, likewise one half
of all rest of my Moveable Effects, and one half of the cash....
sons Samuel and James, Exrs., 4 January 1780
Wit: Jno Douglass
    Samuel Boyd   Jno. Scot (Seal)
    John Boyd
    John Sharpton (E)
Probated on 23d day of November 1782 on the oath of Samuel Boyd, before
John Ewing Colhoun, Esqr., Ordinary of the District of Ninetysix.

53-54 South Carolina, Ninetysix District, October the Second, 1782.
Will of Solomon Hendcock, being very sick....
to my son William Hencock, 300 acres of land, the Plantation whereon I
now live, and one Negro Boy named Harrey, and one Feather Bed & Furniture; to my son Richard, one Negro Jack, and two Hogsheads of Tobacco;
to my Daughter Sarah Hencock, three Negroes Tamer, Joe and Tab, and
one Bald-Eagle Mare, branded on shoulder and Buttock M, also one Loom
and Gears, and Choise of the Beds; to my sons William & Richard Hencock, one Negro Boy named Isaac; to my Daughter Ann Hill, twenty Shillings sterling, one negro woman Sarah, during her life and then to be
the property of Elisha Hill her son, and the lawful begoten heirs of
his Body,if none heirs at his Death, the property to belong to the
Next youngest son Daniel Hill; to my daughter Elizabeth Cox, one Negro
Woman named Jude and her increse; remainder of estate to be divided
to my son William Hencock, my son Richard Hencock, and my Daughter
Sarah Hencock; my son John Gorre Senr to be my Exr.
Test: Daniel Gorre
    Noah Bonds (N)   Solomon Hencock (X) (Seal)
    Richard Bonds (RB)
Probated 23d day of November 1782 on the oath of Daniel Gorre, before
John Ewing Colhoun, Esqr., Ordinary of the District of Ninetysix.

54   State of South Carolina)
       Ninetysix District   ) Be it Remembred that in the Night of the
                                      fourth day of this Instent- we to wit John
Foster, John Cozbey, and Margaret McCarter, being each of us present
in the Dwelling House of James Foster in the Long Cane Settlement in
Said District, the said James Foster being then in his last sickness
of which he died, on Monday night following being the Sixth instant,
that in the night first mentioned the said James Foster, appeared to
us to be of perfect Memory and understanding, The said James Foster
told the said John Foster, that he would wish to settle his affears
as he belived it was Death that was Working with him & therefore desired his father, said John Foster, to bring the above John Cozbey,
present that he might declear before them both how he would desire his
affears to be ordered, the above Margaret McCarter, being also present
with us & in the presence of the said James Foster, who desired his
lands might be divided between his four sons, viz, John Foster, James
Foster, Robert & Samuel Foster, to wit, one hundred acres of land to
each of his said sons, that his Eldest son John, was to have 100 acres
at a place called the five Springs, that his Son James was to have his
100 acres at a place Called the Spring, which the said witnesses under-

stood, to be next adjoining to the five Springs above mentioned but did
not direct how the Remaining 200 acres of land where his Dwelling House
was, how it should be divided between his two youngest sons viz Robert
and Samuel. The said James Foster, being desired by his father, John
Foster, to Consider who he would order matters between & Concerning his
wife and Daughter, made a pause for sometime, but his sickness so in-
creased that afterwards he the said James Foster, was not so Composed
as to be Capable to proceed farther in ordring how his other parts of
property should be settled or disposed of.
10 May 1782
Present: William Clark   John Foster
         Robert Kirkwood   John Cozbey (᭜)
                                              Margaret McCarter (᭜)
Probated on the 6th day December 1782 on the oaths of the above
John Foster, John Cozbey & Margaret McCarter, before John Ewing Colhoun,
Esqr., Ordinary.

55   The will of Jhon(sic) Montgomery, of South Carolina and Ninetysix Dis-
     trict, the fourth day of Janaury 1777....
     to Jane My Dearly beloved wife the Black Mare Called Bleas, and Saddle,
     and Bay Mare Bess; to my dearly beloved Daughter Margaret, the Brown
     Mare called Flie and a Black heffer....to my Dearly beloved Daughter
     Agness, Besses colt and one Rod heffer....likewise to my two daughters
     Jennet and Jane, I give all the remainder of my cattle; to my dearly
     beloved son John, all my Plantation or Tract of Land, and my Bible;
     I allow my Stock of Hogs to go for the support of my family....
     wife Jane, and James Finley & Joseph Pickens, Exrs....
     Wit: Samuel Finley
          Pickens   John Montgomery (Seal)
          Jas. Finley.
     Probated on the oath of Samuel Finley, 13th December 1782.

     [Page 56 is blank]

     [The following are copies of three loose fragments found with the
      foregoing material.]

          During the troubles a certain William Cox who lived in this [   ]
     and always maintained a very good Character, but was a Simple man, and
     being much threatned on account of some Negroes and other property
     that he had honestly acquired by his industry, foolishly went down the
     County about the time that the British left Ninty Six, with a view of
     saving his property from those who had threatned him, he was an old man
     and had never been in arms, and when he went down went and lived under
     the protection of our men on John island till himself and most of his
     family died, Some daughters he left, who brought home his Negroes, the
     eldest of whom is marryed [   ] William Cannon the bearer of this, with
     whose Character I acknowledge myself unaquainted, however as he is
     the most proper person I think to take out letters of administration
     on the estate, and the Brother of the deceased (who has always bore
     the Character of a Simple honest man, and has never been in arms a-
     gainst the Country nor taken part in any way) being [   ] you will
     judge whether it is not properer for them than any other person, who
     may pretend to act on this Occasion. I am with Respect [   ] Sir
                              Your most obed' hble. Servt
                                              James Olephant
                                       Belmont 17th of March 1783
     Colguhant 19
     [reverse:] To John Ewen Coluhoun Esqr
                    by Wm. Canner

Ninetysix)   Personally Came the within Named James Christopher
District)   before me and Made oath That the within Sum of ₤ 500
Currency was the penalty the within named Williams Davis was bound in
to make him lawful Titles for the within mentioned land, and that about
three Months before the date of the within Note he paid the said William
Davis Seventy five pounds in Speice, being the full Consideration pur-
chiase Money That Said Davis is since deceased without making any title
for said land or making him any Satisfection in either part or whole for
the Same
Sworn to the 2d day of September 1782.   James Christopher
before me Pat: Calhoun Jp

know all Men by These present that I William Davis of Nintysix Districk
Do promise to pay or Cause to Be paid unto James Christopher or his
aras or a Sins of the Districk afore Said the full and Jest Sum of
₤ 500 South Carolinah Curency on Condishons the Said Davis Do Not or
Cannot Make a good So fishent Right to a sartin track of land lying
Betwene the Chereke pounds Giving Under My hand this 12th Day of
July 1776   his
                                                William X Davis
                                                        mark

Schedule of Notes etc due the Estate of Alexander Noble Decd.
(Continued)
[List gives only names and amounts, pages are in poor condition, and
 some names are obliterated or merely missing]
William Barksdale, John Barksdale, Peter Bevil, Covington Pemberton,
Ezekiel Coldwell, William Calhoun Jr., Anne Clark, John H. Cofer, Thomas
Casey, A. Calhoun, John Cameron, Joseph Calhoun, John Cain, John P.
Covin, Samuel Currae, Jos. Calhoun, J. Calhoun, Thomas Dickey, Nancy
Davis, John Deall, Peter Downey, Joshua Dubose, H. Darracott, John
Edgar, John L. Weed, Robert Waddel, John Glover, John B. Wingfield,
John Gray, Andrew Willson, George L. Green, Robt M. Harris, Richard
Harris, Linder Hunter, ___ Harris, ___ Hopkins, ___ Hawick, William
Harper, J. Houston, James J. Harris, Jnon. Newby, N. G. Norwood, Ezekiel
Noble, Andrew Norris, Alexander Keown, John King, Nathan Lusk, William
Lee, Jos. Turnbull, Hague Lawton, T. & P Thompson, John Leroy, Thos.
Thompson, Evans H. Taylo, Evans H. Taylor & Co., John H. Morris, J. H.
Mantague, John M. Mathews, F. S. Miller, McKiney & Ward, Vincent Mc-
Elhaney, Richard H. Moseley, Mary Martin, John Macyuns, James McKelny,
David McLin, J. W. McKinsey, Richard Moseley, Mosley & Lesler, George
Mahoney, Thos. Mayn, V. McElhaney & J. Robinson, Wm Robinson, Duke
Smith, Alexander Meres, Benjamn. H. Saxon.

END

INDIANS
Capuchey 44
Delia 43
Indian Peter 44
Indian Prince 45
Metawney 42, 43, 44, 47, 48, 49
Nitehuckey 41
Rose 41, 42, 49

MULATTOS
Amy 37
August 42
Betsey 41, 43, 46, 49
Clarissa 48
Daniel 37
Mall 37
Mulatto Dick 38
Rachel 31, 43, 46
Sally 44, 48
Sapho 41, 43, 46, 49

MUSTEES
Cela 44
Little Frank 41
Peter 44

NEGRO SLAVES
Abraham (Abram) 44, 45, 51, 58
Acon 28
Adam 34
Agge 33
Allen (Allin) 28, 54
America 33
Amos 38
Andrew 34, 59
Augustine 37
Barbe 37
Barsheba 33
Beck 38
Becky 34, 42
Ben 32, 55
Bess 41
Bett 33, 57
Betty 34, 36, 41, 44, 59
Bidgo 44
Big Dick 59
Billey (Billy) 37, 42, 44, 59
Bob 28, 31, 33, 39, 55, 58
Boub 34
Brass 58
Bridget 35, 37
Brin 48
Brister Jimm 58
Bulley 43
Callo 32
Cassandra 47
Cate (Kate) 34, 43, 55, 56, 59
Cato 41
Celia 37
Cesar 58
Charles 28, 32, 38, 54, 57
Charley 33
Charlotte (Charlot) 37, 44, 46
Charty 28
Chevers 43
Cieley 34
Clark 28
Cleranda (Claranda) 42
Cloe 38, 44, 58
Coboy 42
Coffe 41
Coggo 30
Colopeter 43
Cornelia 41
Cresha 43
Curry 59
Cyrus 37, 44, 58
Darkey 42
Davey 41
Deborah 42
Dick 28, 30, 33, 38, 39, 42
Dido 44
Dinah (Dina) 34, 42, 54, 56, 59
Doll 28, 55
Duncan 33, 57
Dutch Jemmy 42
Edenborough 36
Edmond 28, 54
Edy 28, 59
Elsey (Elcey) 37, 44, 49
Emma 44
Eskes 30
Eve 58
Fanny 34, 51, 59
Fillice (Phillis) 33, 39, 40, 59
Foot 37, 46
Frank 28, 34, 43, 59
French Jemmey 47
French Peter 42
Friday 40, 41, 59
Gabe 39
Gabriel 44
Gadow 59
Georgia Dublin 44
Going 59
Georgia Dublin 44
Going 35
Goodfellow 41
Goodgs 58
Gorge 32
Granville 30
Grays March 42
Gwind Tom 42
Hannah (Haner) 28, 34, 35, 38, 42, 48, 54, 59
Harry 32, 36, 43, 55, 59
Henry 59
Ingston 42
Isaac 32, 33, 36, 51, 59

NEGRO SLAVES - Continued
Jack (Jak) 28, 32, 33, 35, 36, 37, 39, 54, 55, 58, 59
Jacob 37, 44, 46, 55
James 35, 37, 38, 39
Jamey 37
Jane 29, 37, 38, 39, 51, 55
January (Jenary) 30, 58
Jeff 29
Jeffry 59
Jemima (Jamima) 42, 47
Jemmie 58
Jene 30, 59
Jenny 59
Jess 37
Jincy 35
Jinny 35
Joe (Jo) 28, 32, 33, 35, 41, 42, 44, 54, 55, 58, 59
Juba 42
Juda 33, 34
Jude (Judy) 30, 35, 36, 37, 49, 51, 58, 59
Judith 52, 58
Julis 32
Juney 37
Kelly 41, 44
Kelly's Dick 49
Ketch 49
King 43
Kitt 28
Leander 30, 43
Lenday 38
Lett 32, 55
Lewis 35
Lidy (Lyda) 28, 38
Lilley 36
Limerick 43
Little Dick 59
Little Jack 28
Little Jacob 42
Little March Katte 44, 49
Lize 36
Long John 43
Lucky 59
Lucy 28, 33, 34, 36, 41, 49, 55, 58, 59
Lunnen 37
Mager (Major) 35, 59
Marcha 44
Margret 43
Maria 37, 43, 44, 47
Martha 47
Mary 34
May 39
Member 58
Meriot 28
Michal 41
Mill 29
Milly 32, 55

Minerva 44
Ming 49
Mingo (Mengo) 35, 43, 58
Mitley 39
Mode 58
Moll 42, 49
Molley 37, 58, 59
Moriah 54
Morris 38
Moses 32
Nance 33
Nancy 34, 37, 41, 59
Nanny 37, 39, 59
Ned 30, 33, 44, 47, 58
Ned (Cut Nose) 47
Nell 29, 34, 36, 59
Nero 43
New Negro Dick 43
New Negro Jack 43
Ockera 43
Old Cato 37
Old Cyrus 44, 47
Olipher 43
Omey 34
Orange 32
Pahnney 35
Patience 28
Patt 35, 37, 51, 54
Patty 28, 59
Peggy 36
Pery 28
Peter 28, 29, 30, 35, 37, 43, 56, 58, 59
Petersisom 41
Phebe (Phebee) 37, 58
Phels 28
Phil 38
Phina 43
Pindar (Pender) 28, 58
Poll 34
Pompey 36, 41, 59
Ponpon Jemmey 44
Pricila 38
Prince 32, 36, 37
Pumkin 37
Quash 35, 51
Rachel 41
Roben 37
Rockaman 58
Roger 35, 50
Rose (Roase) 34, 37
Ruth 37
Sabira 52
Saff 59
Sam 30, 31, 33, 37, 38, 49, 50, 58
Sanco 33
Santy 35
Sarah (Sary) 28, 32, 35, 37, 41, 42, 43, 58, 59,
Seipio 59

NEGRO SLAVES - Continued

Sely 34
Shus 36
Sib 44
Sillas 28
Silvey 54
Simon 48, 58
Singaric 28
Solomon 34, 36, 59
Squash 52
Stephen 33, 39
Stepney 28, 43
Sue (Sew) 33, 37, 42, 44, 55, 58
Syefa 41
Sylvea (Silvia) 28, 35, 37, 42
Tab 32
Tamer 28, 32
Tennah 38
Theeney 36
Tina (Tiney) 38, 42, 49
Tinner 52
Tom 30, 34, 36, 41
Tomb 34
Toney (Tony) 30, 59
Trump 38, 42
Tupter 29
Venus 31, 58
Vienace 38
Warick 44
Wenn 54
Will 37, 54
Wine 29
Winny 38
York 58
Young Sib 44, 49

Abel (Abele), Joseph 18, 23, 32, 55
Abney, Samuel 3, 51
Adams, Benjamin 50, 51
Adams, Coweatling 40
Adams, Drury 3, 35, 50, 51
Adams, Elisabeth 8, 35, 51
Adams, Jacob 40
  James 3, 35, 50
  James, Jr. 8, 35, 51
  Littlebury 50, 51
  Rachel 51
  Rebekah 9, 51, 53
  Sarah 50, 51
  Thomas 3, 50, 51
Adkins, Joseph 29
Agny, William 28
Akins, Joseph 32
Alexander, David 37
  George 33
  Robert 10, 53
  William 25, 56
Allberten see Allbritton
Allbritton, John 25, 57
Allen, James 6, 18, 35
  Josiah 6, 35
  Sherwood 29
Allin see Allen
Allison, Richard 3, 28, 51
  Thomas 29
Anderson, Abel 23
  Charity 9
  Gabrill 20, 58
  John 2, 33, 49
  Rebekah 31
  Robert 11, 33
  Samuel 8, 33, 35, 36, 40
  William 3, 23, 29, 51
Appleton, Thomas 12, 35
Ardeis, Mrs. Christian 3
  Mathias 3
Ashford, George 30
Atkins, Alexander 46
  Widow 46
  William 46
Aubrey, Chandler 21
Bacon, Nathl. 30
Bages, John 11
Baker, James 38
Barksdale, Beverly 29
Barksdale, John 61
  Richard 15
  William 61
Barlow, Robert 40
Barnard, ___ 45
  Edward 37
  Jane 37
  Timothy 46, 48
  William 37
Barronton, James 40
Barwick, Simon 8
Baskins, James 1

Baxter, William 35
Bayley, Elijah 40
Beal, Mary 15, 16
Beckum, Reuben 17, 29
  Russel 17
  Thomas 17, 29
Bell, Henry 37
  John 39
  Robert 6
  Samuel 28
  Thomas 33
  William 33
Bender, George 13, 57, 58
Bennit, John 22, 29
Benson, William 34
Bentley, Joseph 37
Benton, Lewis 29
Berrey, George 24, 26
  William 26
Bevil, Peter 61
Bird, Benjamin 37
Blackey, Benjamin 26
Blacklard, Johannes 29
Bledsoe, Bartelet 26
Blith, John 38
Bob, William 33
Bogan, James 15, 25, 57
Bole, John 39
Bond, Bazall 14
Bond(s), Noah 22, 59
Bond(s), Richard 22, 32, 59
Bond, Robert 1, 6, 20
Bowers, David 10, 13, 37
Bowman, Jacob 10, 29
  Sarah 10, 29
Box, Joseph 29
Boyd, Agnes 50
  John 21, 59
  Mary 50
  Robert 1, 2, 3, 36, 50
  Robert, Jr. 3, 50
  Samuel 21, 59
  William 50
Boyes, Alexander 6, 36, 40
  Arthur 6, 36
Boyl, Charles 40
Braford, Moses 23, 32
Brandon, Thomas 5, 26, 31, 32
Brasswell, David 19, 29
Brawford see Braford
Brayns, Robert 8
Breazeal, Williss 1
Brewer, James 22, 29
Broadaway, Charles 29
Brooks, Elisha 4, 35, 40
  Frances 4, 35
Brown, Benjamin 29
  Hugh 29
  John 29
  Richard 37
  Squire 57
  William 1, 9, 28, 39

Brunsten, Samuel 37
Bryan, John 22
  Robert 34, 36
  Sarah 36
Bryant, Robert 4
  Sarah 4
Buckhalter, Michael 29, 35
Bulow, Joachim 12, 13, 35
Burdit, Averilla 23
Burdit, Giles 23, 29
Burditt see Burdit
Burney, Andrew 3, 21, 57, 58
Burroughs, William 22, 39
Butler, James 18, 36, 40
Butler, Joseph 43
Butler, Patrick 37
Buttler see Butler
Buzbee, Henry 40
Cain, John 61
Caldwell, Betsey 46
Caldwell, David 30
  Ezekiel 61
  James 23, 30, 31, 39
  James, Sr. 26
  John 23, 29, 30, 35, 55
  Mary 46
  William 23, 30
  William Thomas 26
Calhoun, A. 61
  Hugh 50
  J. 61
  John 31
  Capt. John 6, 19, 36
  John, Sr. 6, 36
  John Ewing 1, 24, 36, 37, 38, 39, 40, 49, 50, 51, 58, 59, 60
  Joseph 28, 61
  Patrick 1, 2, 11, 14, 16, 27, 28, 29, 30, 31, 32, 33, 34, 35, 36, 37, 38, 39, 40, 50, 51, 52, 53, 54, 56, 57, 61
  William 19, 36, 39
  William, Jr. 61
Callwell see Caldwell
Cameron, John 61
Cammel-Campbel see Campbell
Campbell, Mrs. 46
  Cartan 46
  Jesse 25, 56
  Margaret 56
  William 40
Canner, William 60
Cannon, Thomas 33
  William 26, 60
Carlile, Francis 39
  James 39
Carson, Thomas 28
Carson, William 11, 14, 26, 28

Carter, James 10, 11, 36, 53
  Lettice 11, 36
  Patty 15
  Robert 11, 15, 27, 53
  Sarah 10, 53
  Thomas 10, 11, 15, 29, 36, 53
Casey, Thomas 61
Chalmers, James 38
Chandler, William 31
Cheney, Betsey 5
  James 5
  John 5, 36
  Priceilla 5, 36
Cherry, Moses 15, 31
Chiney see Cheney
Chirry see Cherry
Christopher, James 12, 13, 30, 33, 61
Clark, Alexander 11, 36
  Anne 61
  John 13, 31, 58
  Lewis 19, 34
  William 11, 28, 36, 40, 60
Cobb(s), John 19, 30
  Jude 19, 30
Cochran, John 25, 56
  Rachal 32
Cockbourn, John 52
Cockeroft, Ogdon 40
Cofer, John H. 61
Coffie, William 33
Coil, Thomas 33
Cohran see Cochran
Coldwell see Caldwell
Cone, James 29
Conner, John 34
Coodie, Arthur 12, 30
Coodie, Edeth 12, 30
Cook, John 34, 40
  Mathew 33
Corley, Richard 25, 26
Couch, Edward 40
Court, Edward 9
Covin, John P. 61
Covington, William 30
Cowan, John 11, 36
Cox, Baveley 26
  Elizabeth 59
  John 32
  Mary 11
  William 26, 60
Cozby, Elizabeth 20
Cozby, John 22, 59, 60
Crasswell, George 28
Crawford, Elizabeth 56
  James 56
  James, Sr. 25
  James, Jr. 56
  John 56
  Prudence 1

Crawford, Cont.
  Thomas 56
  William 56
Crossley, George 49
  Henry 49
  Martha 45, 47, 49
  Mary 49
  William 48
Crossly see Crossley
Cunningham, Robert 11, 54
  Thomas 14
Cureton, William 20, 31, 58
Currae, William 20, 31, 58
Currae, Samuel 61
Currey, John 30
Cusach, Warren 52
Cushman, Simeon (Simon) 6, 20, 30
Daniel, James 55
Darby, Benjamin 21
Darby, William 20, 58
Darracott, H. 61
David see Davis
Davies, Mr. 33
Davis, John 7, 10, 37, 52
  Moses 3
  Nancy 61
  Nathaniel 31
  Vachal 30
  William 12, 13, 30, 37, 61
Dawkins, William 31
Dawson, Britton 21, 58
  Joseph 14, 28
Day, Joseph 33
Deall, John 61
DeLoach, Michael 23, 29
DeLouch see DeLoach
Denham, Alexander 35
Denneson, Patrick 41
Derborough, Benjamin 4, 37
  Mary 4, 37
DeVeaux, James 41
Devlin, James 14
DeVori, Matthew 22
Dick, John 2, 37, 50
  Joseph 2, 50
  Mary 2, 37, 50
  Thomas 50
  William 50
Dickey, Thomas 61
Divlen see Devlin
Dobbins, James 14
Doblins see Dobbins
Douglas, John 19, 21, 34, 59
Downen, Josiah 14, 56
Downey, Peter 61
Drennan, Mary 25
  William 1, 25, 39
Dubose, Joshua 61
Duff, Daniel 21
Dugliss see Douglas

Dunbar, William 2, 9, 12, 13, 37, 48
Dunifin, ___ 43
Dupee, John 37
  Rachel 41, 42, 46, 47, 48
Durborough see Derborough
Durowzeaux, Peter 37
Edgar, John 61
Edmingston, David 5
Edwards, Thomas 38
Ekins, John 28
Elliot, William 35
English, Andrew 33
Erwin, Robert 11, 53
Eskridge, Burditt 10, 37, 52
Eskridge, Grigesby 52
  Nance 10, 52
  Richard 52
  Samuel 52
Evans, Daniel 10
  Jemima 10, 37
  Richard 10, 37
Farned, Edwin 8, 37
  Hannah 8
Farr, William 23, 31
Farrow, Thomas 26
Fedrick see Fredrick
Felts, Fredrick 29
Ferned see Farned
Ferrel, James 40
Filpot, Thomas 37
Finley, James 22, 33, 60
Finley, Samuel 22, 33, 60
Ford, Bolden 23
  Sarah 23, 24
Foreman, George 37
  Isaac 21, 30
  Jacob 21, 30
  Rachal 21, 30
Forrester, Stephen 37
Foster, James 22, 59, 60
  John 8, 22, 46, 51, 59, 60
  Moses 8, 51
  Robert 59, 60
  Samuel 35, 59, 60
  Sarah 55
Fowler, William 24
Franklin, Joseph 31
Frasier, Mrs. 46
Frederick, James 19, 31, 32, 39
  John 18, 19, 31, 32, 55
Freeman, Thomas 40
Frair, ___ 49
Fridig, Gabriel 40
Gains, David 40
Galman see Gallman
Gallman, Casper 9
  Conrad 39
  Harmon 8, 9, 39
Galphin, Barbara 41, 44, 45, 47, 48, 49

Galphin, Cont.
  Catherine 45
Galphin(s), George 2, 9, 37,
    41, 42, 43, 45, 47, 48,
    49
  John 2, 42, 43, 44, 45,
    47, 48, 49
Galphin, Judith 42, 43, 44,
    45, 47, 48
  Martha 42, 45, 46, 47, 49
Galphin(s), Thomas 2, 37, 41,
    42, 46, 47, 48, 49
Gendrate, Henry 21, 22
George, David 7, 30
  Rebecca 7, 30
  William 7, 30
Gibson, Mary 14, 28
  Samuel 14, 28, 33
  Thomas 29
Gillispie, Andrew 35
  James 33
  Mathew 33
  William 33
Gillum, Robert 18, 23
Gindrat see Gendrate
Glanton, Benjamin 8, 35, 36,
    40
Glover, Fredrick 54
  John 61
Goggens, James 32
Golding, Anthony 11, 34, 38,
    54, 55
  James 54
  John 3, 16, 51, 55
  Peggey 16, 55
  Reuben 16, 32, 34, 55
  Richard 11, 32, 38, 55
  Robert 55
  William 16, 54, 55
Golightly, Amey 8, 51
  Christopher 51
  Clairmon 51
  David 8, 51
  Mary 51
  William 8, 38, 51
Goling see Golding
Goode, William 25, 33, 57
Goodgion, William 37
Gordon, Cassey 58
  Elizabeth 20, 31, 58
  George 31, 58
  John 58
  Posey 58
  Thomas 20, 31, 32, 58
  William 20, 31, 58
Gore see Gorre
Gorre, Daniel 21, 32, 59
  James 20
  John, Sr. 22, 32, 59
Gorman, John 30, 31, 39
Graham, John 2, 47
Grasty, Ann 7

Grasty, Cont.
  Sharshall (Charchell) 7, 38
Gray, John 5, 36, 39, 41, 42,
    61
  Joshua 9, 40
Grear, Joseph 24
Green, Bryan (Briant) 22, 29
  George L. 61
  John, Sr. 17
  John Jr. 17
  William 31
Greenaway, John 37
Grey see Gray
Grierson, Mr. 46
  Mrs. 46
  George 48
  James 48
Griffen see Griffin
Griffen, Anthony 11, 38
  Fanny 16
  James 16, 55
  John 22
  Milley 55
  Richard 11, 23, 30, 32,
    34, 38
  William 22, 37
Griffith, James 28
  Margaret 56
  William 56
Griffitt see Griffith
Grigsby, Enoch 7, 10, 35, 36,
    37, 52
  James 26
  Millenr. 26
Grisset, John 28
Guinn, Morris 35
Habersham, James 37
Hairston, Thomas 17, 31
  William 17, 18, 31
Hall, Alexander 35
  James 14, 38
  John 40
  Martha 37
  Mary 14, 38
  William 14
Halloway, Ruben 28
Hallum, James 56
  Jenney 14, 38, 56
  John 14
  Josiah 56
  Martha 56
  Thomas 56
  William 14, 38, 56
Halveston, Philip 37
Hamilton, Andrew 15
  William 31
Hammeger, James 33
Hammond(s), Ann 25
  John, Sr. 24, 25
  Joshua 24, 33
  LeRoy 7, 8, 9
Hampton, Edward 22

Hampton, Cont.
  Sally 22
Hancock, Richard 32, 59
  Sarah 32, 59
  Solomon 21, 32, 59
  William 31, 32, 59
Handcock see Hancock
Hankinson, Robert 2, 37
Harding, William 2, 49
Harper, William 61
Harris, ___ 61
  Benjamin 33
  James 39
  James J. 61
  Rev. Mr. John 1, 8, 20
  Richard 61
  Robert M. 61
  Thomas 6
  William 35
Harrison, Charles 40
  James 8, 9, 35, 36, 40
Hartle, Daniel, Sr. 40
Hartly, Frederick 40
Harvey, John 7
  Michael 12
  Thomas 7
Harwick, James 20, 31
Hatcher, Joab 33
Hatcher, Thomas 33
Hawick, ___ 61
Hawkens, Pinketham 12
Hay---Hays
Hayles, Adam 10
Hays, Alice (Elcie) 18, 31
  Charles 33
  Henery 33
  Joseph 18, 32
  Milliam 1, 2, 3, 36, 39, 50
Heard, Charles 28
  George 30
Hearst, Ann 53
  Christian 53
  Elizabeth 53
  George 53
  John 11, 28, 33, 38, 53
  Joseph 53
  Margaret 53
  Mary 11, 53
  Robert 53
  Thomas 53
  William 53
Hencock-Hencoch see Hancock
Henderson, Richard 2, 49
Hendricks, Isaac 38
Herd see Heard
Herendon see Herndon
Herndon, John 3, 8, 9, 51
  Ruth 52
Hews see Hughs
Higgans, John 40
Hiles, Adam 13, 33, 37
Hill, Adam 29

Hill, Cont.
  Ann 32, 59
  Daniel 59
  Elisha 59
  William 30, 39
Hinton, Allen 12, 30
  Robert 29
Hodge, Benjamin 29
Hogans, James 7, 39
Hogg, Frances 58
  James 58
  John 20, 31, 58
  Joseph 58
  Lewis 20, 31, 58
  Sarah 20, 58
  Stephen 58
  Thomas 58
  Zachariah 58
Hoggwood (Hagewood), William 28
Holland, Charles 38
Hollensworth, Elias 5, 7, 14, 20, 21, 23, 26
  Jeptha 25, 57
Hollinger, Titus 37
Holly, Nicholas 38
Holms, David 45, 48
  Margret 45
  Robert 45
  Thomas 49
  William 49
Horry, Jonah 2, 48
Houston, J. 61
Howell, Nathaniel 37
Hughes see Hughs
Hughs, Demsey 17, 29
  Elizabeth 23, 32
  John 23, 29, 32, 57
  Joseph 5, 31, 57
  Mary 5, 57
  Richard 25, 57
  William 5, 31, 57
Humphreys, Jane 53
Hunter, Linder 61
Hutson, David 7
Irvin, David 37
Irwin, John 31, 36
Issom, Abigier 6
Issom, Edward 6, 38
Jackson, John 28
  Walter 52
James, Charles 8, 51
Jefferson, Joseph 29
Johnson see Johnston
Johnston, Benjamin 10, 53
  Catherine 11, 54
  Daniel 31
  Howell 18, 31, 32, 39, 40, 55
  James 10, 25, 53, 57
  John 11, 21, 32, 33, 40, 54
  Richard. Sr. 40

Johnston, Cont.
  Sarah 21, 32
  Thomas 32
Jones, Danial 33
  Francis 27
  Henry 10, 29, 37
  John 40
  Robert 29
  Thomas 39
  William 3, 7, 9, 10, 37
Jordon, John 38
Kee(s), Thomas 12, 17, 21, 22, 24, 25, 26
Kennedy, John 35
  William 5, 15, 25
Keown, Alexander 61
Key, Henry 33
Kiles, Barney 29
Killgore (Kilgore) Benjamin 24
Killy, James 31
Kindel, William 27
King, Averilla 23
  Charles 58
  Henry 23, 29
  James 30
  John 61
Kirkland, James 40
Kirkwood, Robert 60
Kitt, John 29
Kanp, Peter 33
Lamar, Alexander 37
Lareymor, William 40
Lawton, Hague 61
Lee, Andrew 29
  William 61
Leonard, Laughlin 16, 32, 55
  Mary 16, 32, 55
LeRoy, John 61
Lesly, William 33
  William, Jr. 33
Letcher, James 26
  Milley 26
Levins, Richard 40
Lewis, David 34
Liles, John 5
  Menis 31
  Willimson 32
Lindsey, James 31
  Samuel 31
Lissly see Lesly
Little, Elizabeth 15
Little, James 1, 2, 15
  William 35
  William, Jr. 15, 38
Liveley, Henry 29
Logan, Alexander 5, 34
  David 5, 34
  John 5, 34
Loggan see Logan
Long, James 35
  Martha 56
Lott, Jesse 19, 31, 32, 40

Lott, Cont.
  Sarah 19, 31, 32, 40
Love, Mark 26
Lovless, Benjamin 40
Lowrey, William 54
Luckie, John 20
  William 27, 35
Lusk, Nathan 61
McAlpin, John 32, 33
  Robert 14
McCalpin see McAlpin
McCarley, William 38
McCarter, Margaret 22, 59, 60
McCleskey, David, Jr. 8
  Issabella 8
  James 8
  Joseph 33
McClinton, Robart 32
McClure, William 1
McCluskey, Joseph, Sr. 35
McComb, John 33
McCord, John 15, 18
McCurdy, John, Jr. 35
McDavid, Patrick 24
McDavid, Roseana 24
McElhaney, Vincent 61
McElwee, William 38
McFarland, Lettice 11, 36
McFaron, James 32
McFatrick, John 57
McGill, James 3, 11, 38, 54
McGillvery, Lauchlin 2, 41, 47, 48
McHenry, James 41, 42
McIlveney, John 33
McJunkin, Samuel 15, 25
McKay, Daniel 30
McKeer, William 3
McKeown, George 15
  Tabitha 14
McKenley see McKinley
McKinley, James 22, 39, 61
  William
McKinsey, J. W. 61
McLin, Mr. 29
  David 61
McLine see McLin
McMaster, John 1
  Patrick 1, 3, 50
  William 1
McMillin, Mathew 28
McMurdie, Henry 35
McMurtray, Samuel 1, 31
McQueen, Alexander 46
  John 46
Macyuns, John 61
Maddin, Laughlin 29
Mahoney, George 61
Mann, Samuel 27
  Thomas 38
Manning, Levi 29
Manson, William 27, 35

Mark, Lawrance, Sr. 33
Mark, Patrick 33
Marlen, James 40
Marshall, Joseph 37
Martin, Dr. 33
  Jacob 29
  John 35
  Mary 61
  William 32
Mathew see Mathews
Mathews, Isaac 24
  John M. 61
  Phillep 35
  Victor 36
  William 28
Maxwell, David 4
  John 27, 57
  Nicholas 27, 57
  Robert 18, 27, 33, 57
  William 27, 57
Mayfield, John 25
  Mary 25
Mayn, Thomas 61
Mayson (Mason), George 29
  James 37
Mecklen, Rev. Robert 27
Megin, Daniel 30
Melton, Robert 40
Melvill, Mary 27, 57
  Robert 27, 33, 57
Meres, Alexander 61
Meyer (Mayer) Michael 2, 33, 37, 47
Middleton, Hugh 8, 9, 12, 21, 27
Miles, Aqulea 12
Miller, Andrew 33
  F. S. 61
  John 33, 57
  Joseph 10, 37
Milling, Elisabeth 57
  N. 3
Mills, Henry 37
Minter, John 33
Mitchall, Benjamin 30
Mitchall, Isaac 30
Moat, Andrew 33
Montague, J. H. 61
Montgomery, Agness 33, 60
  James 18, 24
  Jane 60
  Jennet 60
  John 22, 32, 33, 60
  Margaret 60
Moore, Andrew 34
  Anne 16, 22, 54
  Davis 54
  James 16, 28, 40, 54
  John 1, 16, 54
  Jonathan 54
  Patrick 22
  Richard 16, 54

Moore, Cont.
  Sarah 1
  Susanna 54
  William 1, 3, 4, 7, 10, 11, 14, 16, 17, 28, 54
  William, Jr. 14
  Wm. Drayton 54
Morris, John H. 61
Morrow, Arther 3
Moseley & Lester 61
  Benjamin 3, 51
  Hannah 3, 51
  Richard H. 61
  William 52
Mountgomery see Montgomery
Murfey see Murphy
Murphy, Drury 11, 30
  Thomas 24
Murray, John 6, 9, 12, 13, 20, 21, 37
  William 32
Nail, Casper 35
  John 13, 55
  Robert 24
  William 16, 29, 54
Neely, Christopher 54
Nelson, Samuel 35
Netherclift, ___ 46
Newby, Jnon. 61
Newman, Alexander 2, 37, 50
  Ann 2, 50
  George 37, 45
  John 2, 44, 46, 47, 50
Nicholson, David 10, 26, 37
  Wright 23, 29
Nickelson see Nicholson
Noble, Alexander 1, 19, 26
  Ezekiel 61
Noble, James
Noble(s), John 4
  Joseph 52
Nolin, George 48, 49
Norrell, Elizabeth 51
  Isaac 3
  Jacob 51
  James 3, 28, 51
  Levy 51
  Martha 51
  Mary 3, 51
Norris, Agness 18, 55
  Andrew 61
  Elizabeth 18, 55
  John 15
  William 18, 38, 55
Norwood, N. G. 61
Nunn, Joseph 36
O'Bryan, Elener 53
O'Neal, Henry 11, 54
  William 11, 54
Oats, William 37
Odam, Abram 37
  Isaac 37

Odam, Cont.
  Mich. 37
Odam (Odom), Owen 39
Olephant, James 60
Orr, William 26
Otterson, Samuel 21, 32
Owens, Elizabeth 15
  John 15
Palmer, Joshua 15, 25, 57
Pardue, Lilleston 30
Pardue, Field 40
Parker, John 29
Parkinson, John 2, 47
Parsons, George 46
  James 2, 47
Parten, Jesse 40
Patterson, James 32
  Robert 28
Pattigrew see Pettigrew
Patton, Arthur 2, 39
  Samuel 2, 39
Paxton, Samuel 8, 39
Pearson, Henry 16, 18
Pelman, Buckner 40
Pemberton, Covington 61
Perdue see Pardue
Perry, Isaac 37
Perry, Joseph 37
Perry, Penelope 20, 58
  Thomas 20, 58
Person see Parsons
Pettigrew, Ebenezer 8
  Gorge 35
  John 8
Peycock, Henry 33
Philpote, James 29
Pickens, Andrew 33
Pickens, Dakos (Darkos?) 55
  Israel 7, 19, 33, 35
  John 33
  Joseph 33, 60
  Robert 55
  William 33
Pickett, Mille 25, 57
  Thomas 25, 57
Pigg, John 37
Pines, Edward 40
Pinson, Duke 29
Pooler, Quinton 46
Pooler, Quinton 46
Pope, Solomon 7, 10, 16, 18,
  19, 23, 26
Potts, George 11, 54
Prat, William 25
Preter see Pretter
Pretter, John 14, 56
Price, Mary 35
Prichard, James 40
Pursel, John 29
Purvas see Purvis
Purves see Purvis

Pruvis, John 3, 9, 26, 33,
  39
Rae, Thomas 37, 41, 42
Rainsford, John 8, 9, 10, 37,
  53
Rambo, Benaja 52
  Elender 52
  Elizabeth 52
  Joseph 52
  Laurence (Laurens) 9, 52, 53
  Margaretta 52
  Mary 52
  Rebecca 52
  Reuben 52, 53
Rankin, George 46
Raton, John 46
Rattam, John 37
Ray, James 24, 33
Readin, Joseph 58
Red, Job 40
  John 40
Rees, Ephraim 39
Reed see Reid
Reid, George 6, 36, 40
  Hugh 33
Revelin, John 15
Reynolds, Thomas 25, 57
Reynolds, William 25, 34, 57
Rice, Joseph 9, 39
Richardson, Abraham 24, 33
Richey, John 18, 30
Rivers, John 40
Robson-Robenson see Robinson
Robinson, Ann 15
  Clotworthy 2, 47, 48, 49
  J. 61
  John 40
  Joseph 15
  Randal 5, 7
  William 37, 61
Roebuck, John 9, 53
Roquemore, James 40
Rosamond, Samuel 10, 14, 56
Ross, Andrew 26, 32
Roundtree, Jesse 6, 20, 30, 33
  Jethro 6, 33
Ruff, George 5, 7, 22
Runnolds see Reynolds
Russell, Dr. Timothy 33
Rutherford, Robert 31
Ryen, Lecon 30
Salters, Christopher 40
  John 40
Samuel, Elisha 15, 28
Sansom, Jane 5, 34
  John 5, 34
Satterwhite, Bartlett 23, 30,
  35
Sawgens see Sawyers
Sawyers, John 40
Saxon, Benjamin H. 61

Saxon, Cont.
  James 7
Scott, James 21, 40, 59
  John 21, 34, 58
  Samuel 21, 34, 59
Seawritht, James 6, 33, 36, 40
Selfrige, Robert 33
Sallers see Sellers
Sellers, John 37, 43
Sennard, ___ 46
Settles, Francis 37
Seymor, Person (Parson?) 46
Sharp, John 27, 28
  Patty 15, 27, 28
Sharpton, John 21, 59
Shaw, ___ 41
  Catharine 37
  Daniel 6, 20, 33, 35, 40, 41
Shinholser, Catherine 13, 55
  John 13, 29
  William 12, 13, 55
Shoemat, Daniel 40
Short, Hugh 37
Simpson, Margaret 27
  William 27
Sims, Charles 31
Sisson, Frederick 7
  William 7, 10, 18, 35, 36, 37
Smith, Andrew 57
  Duke 61
  Elisabeth Marble 27
  Jacob 10, 37, 52
  James 32, 52
  Joseph 56
  Sarah 10, 52
  Stephen 2, 37
  Thomas 31, 57
  William Bassett 57
Smithers, Christopher 13, 33, 55
  Gabriel 28
  James 55
Smothers see Smithers
Sparks, William 20, 58
Spears, Abraham 37
Spraggins, Nathaniel 3, 7, 51
  Thomas 5
Sprott, John 25, 56
Stalmaker, Samuel 40
Stark, Robert 7, 40, 52
  Samuel 33
Starns, Ebenezer 9, 29, 40
Stedham, Benjamin 45, 48
  Sarah 8
Steel, Aaron 6, 20, 33
Sterk see Stark
Stevens, Shedrak 33
Stewart, John 36
  Samuel 40
Stocks, Bentley 40

Strain, David 24
  James 24
  John 1, 24, 33
  Samuel 24
  Thomas 1, 39
  William 33
Stran see Starns
Strother, Francis 23
Strouble, Gasper 37
Stubbs, Peter 1, 2, 11, 14, 36, 39
Stubes-Stertes see Stubbs
Sturzennegger, John 2, 10, 13, 29, 33, 37, 47, 49, 55
Summeral, Hall 50
Sutherland, Francis 27
Tannes, John 38
Taylor, Mrs. 45
  Evans H. 61
  Henney (Henny) 5, 39
  John 5, 39
Ternigin, Jesse 29
Terry, Champ 28, 29
  Stephen 33
Teulon, Charles 11, 53
Theaker, Joel 33
Thomas, Daniel 5
  James 5, 34, 36
  John, Jr. 9, 11, 14, 21, 24, 27, 28, 36
  Joseph 34
  William 5
Thompson, James 35
  P. 61
  T. 61
  Thos. 61
  William 34, 40
Thomson see Thompson
Tilman, Lewis 35
Timmons, John 34
Tindsley-Tinley see Tinsley
Tinsley, Elizabeth 18, 34, 55
  Golding 18
  Isaac 18, 34
  William 38
Tobler, J. N. 57
  John 13, 29, 33, 55
  Ulric 57
Tomkins, Samuel 40
Towles, Jane 5
  Joseph 4
  Olipher 5
Towns, John 20, 31
  John, Jr. 20, 31
Tork see Turk
  William 32, 38
Turnbull, Elizabeth 56
  Joseph 25, 56, 61
Turner, John 5, 36
Tutt, Benjamin 4, 8, 40
Tylor, Abraham 39

Tylor, Cont.
  Elisha 39
Tyner, Demsey 33
  William 29
Vann, Edward 12, 30
Venable, Joseph 17
Verner, John 35
  Thomas 37
Vernor see Verner
Virden, Eg. 31
Waddel, Robert 61
Wade, ___ 41
  Hezekiah 37, 42
Wadlington, William 31
Wafer, Thomas 20, 58
Waldrop, James 16, 18
Walker, George 37
  Joel 43
  Samuel 30, 39
Wallace, Izabel (Issable) 4, 40
  John 4, 15
  Robert 4, 40
Walsh, Michal 2, 49
Ward, Michael 40
Wardlaw, Hugh 6, 10, 18, 19
  John 1
Warren, Dr. 29
  George 40
  James 40
Wasdon, Elijah 37
Waters, Philemon 18, 19
Watson, Arthur 7, 40
Watson, Eliga 52
  Jacob 40
  John 40
  John, Sr. 9
  John, Jr. 40
  Lewis 40
  Martha 7, 40, 52
  Michael 7, 40, 52
  Richman 7, 52
  Willis 40
Wattes, Thomas 37
Weaver, Aaron 19, 34
  Jane (Jenney) 19, 34
Webb, Henley 40
Weed, John L. 61
Weems, Bartholomew 33
  Thomas 40
Wharton, Samuel 10
White, Henry 8
  John 19, 21, 34, 35
  Joseph 40
  William 19, 20, 35
Whitefield, George 11
Wilkisson, Edward 28
Willard, John 29
  Martin 29
Williams, Celia 9, 40
  Charles 9, 40
  Elizabeth 26
  Gardner 40

Williams, Cont.
  James 55
  Joseph 29
  Lud 13, 21, 55
  Samuel 4, 40
Williamson, Genl. Andrew 33, 57
Wilson, Andrew 61
  George 33
  James 6, 16, 40
  John 6, 36, 40
  Joseph 57
  Martha 6, 40
  Robert 11, 53
  Russell 7, 10, 18, 19, 29,
    34, 35, 36
  Thomas 16, 28, 37
  William 16, 54
Wimberly, Henry 37
Wimbish, Samuel 11, 36
Wingfield, John B. 61
Withers, William R. 7, 52
Wood(s), James 17, 34
  John 17, 34, 37
  Mary 17, 34
  Peter 23
  Rebecca 17, 34
  Thomas 29, 40
Wright, Jacob 29
  Sarah 29
  William 20
Wyld(s), John 3, 4, 11, 16,
    17, 18
Wyley, Mr. 46
  Mrs. 46
  Henry 33
  Suckey 46
Young, ___ 47, 48
Young, John 32, 34
  Robert 33
Zimmerman, Mr., Sr. 33
Zulby, John Joachim 42
  David 2, 12, 13, 33, 35,
    37, 47, 48
  David, Senr. 58
  David, Jr. 21

Index prepared by:
  Marguerite L. Clark,
    Shannon, Miss.

www.ingramcontent.com/pod-product-compliance
Lightning Source LLC
Chambersburg PA
CBHW050606300426